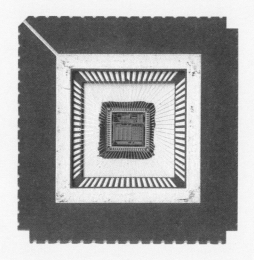

This book is dedicated to Alasdair Thomas (1962-1992)

First edition published by ARM Ltd. 2015

Thanks to Nick Flaherty and Peter Silverton for contributions to the text. Thanks to John Biggs, Pete Harrod, Dave Jaggar, Mike Muller, Lee Smith, Stuart Waldron and the 25x25 contributors for their photographs. All images ©ARM Ltd except the following: p10 (top left) Tim Boyle/Bloomberg via Getty Images/p19 SSPL/Getty Images/p28 ©Universal/ courtesy Everett Collection/Rex Features/p30 Ann E. Yow-Dyson via Getty Images/ p36 Photo 12/UIG/Getty Images/p45 (left) James Keyser/The LIFE Images Collection/ Getty Images/p45 (right) SSPL/Getty Images/p50-51 John Biggs/p74 and p159 By krystof.k (Twitter) & nmuseum (own work)[GFDL(http://www.gnu.org/copyleft/fdl.html) via Wikimedia Commons/p80 Newsmakers/Getty Images/p81 JOKER/Martin Magunia/ ullstein bild via Getty Images/p88 YOSHIKAZU TSUNO/AFP/Getty Images/p99 Justine Hunt/The Boston Globe via Getty Images/p104 Neil Godwin/Guitarist Magazine via Getty Images/p109 Ulrich Baumgarten via Getty Images/p126 SeongJoon Cho/Bloomberg via Getty Images/p132 ROBERTO SCHMIDT/AFP/Getty Images/p147 7831/Gamma-Rapho via Getty Images/p148 © Britta Pedersen/dpa/Corbis/p154 © BlueFrogRobotics/ Splash/ Splash News/Corbis/p155 Jane Phillimore/CCH/p157 © STEVE MARCUS/Reuters/Corbis

Created for ARM Ltd by Essential Works Ltd

ISBN: 9781906615956

Printed in Malta by Gutenberg Press

www.arm.com

ARM25

Contents

Introduction
Back to the Future

The story of ARM begins in the early 1980s, with technology that is now iconic to a generation of engineers: the BBC Micro. This was an 8-bit home computer, sponsored by the BBC and made by a Cambridge-based company called Acorn Computers. The original design had been developed around the 6502 microprocessor by among others Sophie Wilson and Steve Furber, and put together quickly to win a prestigious contract for an educational program being run by the BBC. Sophie and Steve had been friends at the Cambridge University Processor Group, an English version of the Homebrew Club at Stanford University in California, where Steve Jobs and Steve Wozniak of Apple had first met. Sophie and Steve were among the first to work for Acorn at their offices off the market square in the center of Cambridge.

Following the success of the BBC Micro, Acorn was looking for a lower-cost computer to expand the market. The next-generation system, the Electron, used a similar architecture to the original BBC Micro but reduced the design from 102 chips to just 12 by using a large uncommitted logic array, an early gate array technology, which allowed a standard array of logic elements to be programmed in the factory with one metal mask. This allowed a new chip to be designed and manufactured much faster and more cheaply than a full custom design. Despite the simplicity, the Electron would mark a dramatic change in the prospects for Acorn, and indirectly led to the creation of ARM the company.

Soon, Acorn were looking for a new processor to replace the aging 6502. They had been considering using Intel's i286 processor, but Intel was not interested in supplying Acorn with chips. So Steve and Sophie traveled the world looking at the different options for a new processor, including a visit to hundreds of engineers in Haifa who were designing the next processor for National Semiconductor's NS16032, and hundreds more in the US who were working on the 68020 for Motorola. But they weren't impressed with the options available, as they all required complex systems which made them too expensive. In 1983 they visited the Western Design Center in Phoenix, Arizona, where they met one of the designers of the 6502 they had used in the BBC Micro, Bill Mensch. It turned out to be an inspiring and serendipitous visit, because Hermann Hauser, who'd done his own traveling the world in search of

LEFT The future arrived with the release of Acorn's BBC Micro computer in December 1981. Acorn's art department was clearly influenced by progressive rock LP covers of the previous decade.

ABOVE   The Motorola DynaTAC 8000X; the first commercially available (at $4,000) mobile telephone, 1983.

RIGHT   Steve Furber's original hand-drawn layout for the ARM1 chip, 1983. A multibillion-dollar industry owes its existence to this sketch.

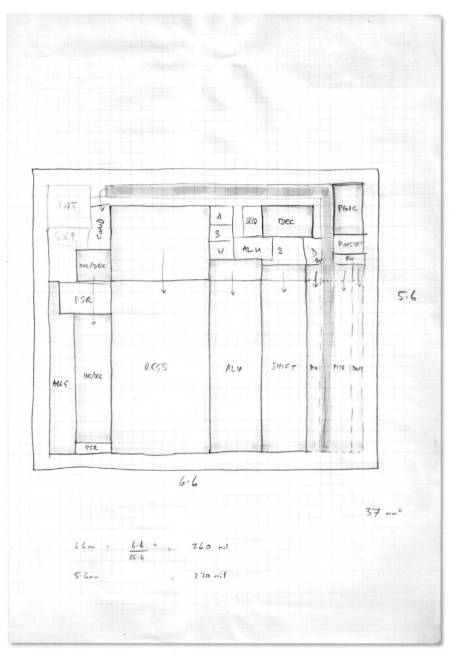

solutions to Acorn's problem, had heard about something called RISC — Reduced Instruction Set Computing — developed at the University of California, Berkeley, with David Patterson (and down the road at Stanford University by John Hennessey), and used for higher performance processor designs by the likes of IBM and Hewlett-Packard. Rather than have complex instructions that are broken down in the processor, the RISC architecture uses a set of simpler instructions, each of which can do less so requires more of them to accomplish the same task. The simplicity of the instruction set is more than compensated for by the increase in speed brought about by the less complicated design.

A lot of companies were working on this technology: Sun Microsystems was developing the SPARC processor, Intel had its i960, HP was underway with its PA-RISC,

25 × 25 Steve (Stephen) Byram Furber

1 Who or what did you want to be when you grew up?   Early years: train driver. Later: airline pilot.

2 What or who was your first obsession?   Model aircraft.

3 Who was your childhood hero (or is now)?   Steve Zodiac (Fireball XL5).

4 What's your secret?   That would be telling ...

5 *Star Trek* or *Star Wars*?   I enjoy both, despite them both violating my scientific sensibilities. *2001: A Space Odyssey* is my favourite of this genre. OK, if forced to choose, *Star Wars*!

6 Did any book change your life? If so, what was it?   Not really.

7 Favorite movie: *Those Magnificent Men in Their Flying Machines* (1965).

8 If you could hear only one piece of music again, what would it be?   *Nights in White Satin*, the Moody Blues. (Obviously!)

9 Vinyl, cassette, 8-track, CD, MP3, or streaming?   MP3.

10 What do you prefer: Skype conference call or face-to-face meeting?   That depends ... I prefer face-to-face unless that involves travel.

11 Your favorite ARM product is: ARM2aS. Was that ever an ARM product?

12 The best use of an ARM product is: iPhone.

13 The best use of an ARM product would be ...   *The Hitchhiker's Guide to the Galaxy*.

14 If you could bring anything back from extinction, what would it be?   Politeness in public affairs.

15 Your favorite mode of transport is ...   Train.

16 What future invention would you like to make (or witness)?   Machine consciousness.

17 Ready, Aim, Fire, or Ready, Fire, Aim?   Ready, Aim, Fire.

18 If you could ask one question of anybody, what would it be and to whom?   Dunno, really. Alan Turing: 'was it an accident or suicide?'

19 When were you happiest? I don't really do ups and downs that much; as get older I am generally increasingly content with my lot.

20 What makes you angry?   Human cruelty to other humans. Airport security queues. Bureaucracy.

21 What does love feel like?   There's nothing that it is remotely comparable with. Except, possibly, chocolate ...

22 Bitcoin or dollars?   Dollars.

23 How much is enough?   Enough to stop worrying about paying the bills but not so much to start worrying about investments.

24 What is your greatest achievement?   ARM1 first silicon working.

25 Beach or adventure holiday?   Adventure.

YEAR OF BIRTH   1953

COUNTRY OF BIRTH   UK

CITY OF RESIDENCE   Manchester

UNIVERSITY + DEGREE
Cambridge: BA Maths (1974), PhD Aerodynamics (1980), MMath (2011)

TENURE AT ARM   Never worked for ARM!

Acorn Computers Limited
Fulbourn Road
Cherry Hinton
Cambridge CB1 4JN

Telephone 0223 245200
Telex 817875 ACORN G
Fax No 0223 210685

Our Ref:JRH/BJM

10th July 1984

Mr D Seal

Dear Dave

As you know, your contract with Acorn and the general law impose upon you
obligations of confidentiality in relation to proprietory information of
the Company (whether of a technical, financial, commercial or other
nature).

I propose to disclose to you certain information about a project
code-named "Project A". You will be one of a very small group within the
Company to receive disclosure of this information. You should be aware
that if this information or even the existence of "Project A" were to
become known outside the Company, it would be extremely damaging to the
Company. I am therefore seeking your written agreement and
acknowledgement that you will not discuss the existence or content of
"Project A" with any person outside the Company or with any person within
the Company who is not part of the "Project A Team". The "Project A Team"
consists of the following persons:

H M Hauser	P B Wynn
C J Curry	J A Merriman
J R Horton	P O'Keeffe
A G McKernan	I L Tibbs
A R Wilson	B J Murphy
S B Furber	M Lee
J B Tansley	D Lamkin
J Dunn	J Thakray
M Muller	H Tyson
R Banerjee	D Seal
A Hopper	T Brown
A Hinchley	B Cockburn
J Mitchell	
C Deller	
M Jordan	

No one may be added to the Project A Team without the specific agreement
of myself, Christopher Curry, Hermann Hauser or Jim Mitchell.

We shall institute specific procedures for ensuring the confidentiality of
Project A and it is your responsibility to be aware of and ensure
compliance with these procedures.

Directors
H M Hauser PhD (Austria)
C J Curry
A Hopper
J R Horton
J A Merriman
P W O'Keeffe
P B Wynn

Registered office
Acorn Computers Limited
Fulbourn Road
Cherry Hinton
Cambridge CB1 4JN
England

Registered No
1403810
VAT No
215 4002 20

The ARM
A Project Proposal

DEVICE SPEC`
                The ARM (Acorn RISC Machine) is a 32 bit reduced
instruction set computer. The concept being a simple data path with 16
32 bit registers, ALU, barrel shifter, and a priority encoder all
controlled by a PLA.
        The ARM is intended to be a simple fast machine.   The result of
this is a chip that will be easier to integrate into systems than a
16032, because it is simpler and needs fewer, less complex, support
chips.   Another benefit is that the ARM can be run at a high speed,
and achieve greater performance both in IO and computation than a
16032.

        PRO'S   CON'S
State of the art technology   It might not work first time
Control of the project   Someone else might do one
Definition of its functionality
We could sell the part
Simplicity means less risk.

                SCHEDULES

IC DEVELOPMENT

    1 yr to 18 months with 2 engineers on the project.

SOFTWARE DEVELOPMENT

    HI-SPEED simulator 2-3 weeks.
    SLOW-SPEED simulator 2-3 weeks.
    ASSEMBLER 2 weeks.

LANGUAGES

Language	Developer	Time	Cost
C & UNIX	Microsoft/Logica	6 Months	25k$
Basic	Acorn	3 Months	---
Pascal,	Lattice Logic	... as 16032 ...	
BCPL,	" "		

FLOATING POINT/MATHS ROUTINES

    We need a numerical algorithms person, who could probably get
these done in 6 months.

APPLICATION PROPOSALS
                        2nd processor.This would enable Acorn to
extensively field trial the part assuming it had the following
configuration:

        +--------+   +------+   +------+
        ! RAM/VM !<------! ARM !<------>! TUBE !
        +--------+   +------+   +------+

            Alvey Workstation

    +------+   +-------------+   +--------+
    ! DISC !<------! I/O custom !------>! VIDEO !
    +------+   +-------------+   +--------+
                        !
                        !
        +------+   +-------------+   +-----+
        ! ARM !<-------------+------>! VM !
        +------+   +-----+

            Low Cost Workstation

    +-----+   +-------------+   +-------------------+
    ! ROM !<------! I/O custom !------>! RAM 512K -> 1M !
    +-----+   +-------------+   +-------------------+
                        !
                        !   +-----+
                        +------>! ARM !
                                +-----+

Obviously the start vehicle should be the second processor and would
take the least of Acorns effort,however to get the most out of the
device a project team could be set up, similar to the 16032 group,that
would drive all products based on the ARM.

The critical decision is which semiconductor company will supply us
with silicon.The part suggests a 2 micron nmos technology and there
are a number of suppliers of this technology, however a couple stand
out as attractive. Hitachi (ACRTC and memory) who we are getting
very close to us and Mullard who are also targeting Acorn.
Another possibility is Honeywell with their ECL technology.

    JOHN UMNEY, ROGER WILSON ,HARRY BARMAN

EOR
!lffffff<!ff!ff!<ff~f
f!ff!lffcwkkcc<ff~fffffv~nff

ABOVE The confidentiality agreement given to the "Project A" team
in July 1984.
RIGHT The initial "Project A" proposal.

IBM had its Power architecture, and Motorola was working on the 88000 — they were all in development at this time. Seeing the commercial sense of RISC, in 1984 Hennessey started a company to capitalize on the idea, and called it MIPS Computer Systems (renamed MIPS Technologies Inc. in 1992, it remains a competitor to ARM).

Sophie and Steve loved the way that Bill's team worked; unlike their competitors, who generally favored a big engineering center employing thousands of engineers, the WDC was a bungalow in a city suburb. Inside, Bill was drawing the design of a processor on a large sheet of paper. "We could do that," they thought, "while developing a RISC processor." Unlike other engineers developing RISC, Sophie and Steve decided that the way to go was to keep things as simple as possible, maintaining a balance between speed and low cost. Everyone else would create RISC designs optimized for speed, but their designs were more complicated, and therefore expensive. The work required would need to be kept under wraps for as long as the development would take, because of a fierce rivalry in the UK computing industry; a letter, headed Project A, was sent by John Horton, Acorn's Technical Director, to the team members involved in the work, stressing the need for confidentiality. Soon after, Sophie came up with the instruction set architecture for what was to become the Acorn RISC machine (ARM). The ARM1 had

ABOVE   The first ARM BBC Micro second processor. The BBC Micro had anticipated the need for future expansion and supported a high speed expansion bus, called the TUBE, which enabled a second processor to be connected which then used the BBC Micro as a high performance IO subsystem.

25 × 25 Sophie Mary Wilson

YEAR OF BIRTH 1957
COUNTRY OF BIRTH England
CITY OF RESIDENCE Cambridge (well, a village just outside)
UNIVERSITY + DEGREE Cambridge: Computer Science
TENURE AT ARM Never joined, only at Acorn and some consultancy for ARM

1 Who or what did you want to be when you grew up? I thought I'd die before I got very old — lots of childhood illness — so never gave it any brain time

2 What or who was your first obsession? I don't think I ever got obsessed (followed one thing to the exclusion of all others) — I'm always interested in lots of different things at any one time

3 Who was your childhood hero (or is now)? None. Possibly for the reasons in 1.

4 What's your secret? My life is now an open book

5 Star Trek or Star Wars? Neil Gaiman's *Stardust*

6 Did any book change your life? If so, what was it? *RCA CMOS IC data book 1972* — reading it led directly to working for Hermann Hauser

7 Favorite movie: Varies with time … Movie I've watched most often is *The Princess Bride*

8 If you could hear only one piece of music again, what would it be? Varies … Just listened to Mike Oldfield's *Hergest Ridge* after walking there, so it might be his *AMAROK* album, which I listened to on a portable CD player while walking an awful lot when it came out. Or it might be Handel's *Music for the Royal Fireworks* or *Water Music*

9 Vinyl, cassette, 8-track, CD, MP3, or streaming? I never had an 8-track and stream very little

10 What do you prefer: Skype conference call or face-to-face meeting? F2F

11 Your favorite ARM product is: ARM1, since without it there wouldn't be the rest of them

12 The best use of an ARM product is: All of them together

13 The best use of an ARM product would be … Dr McCoy's (if I spelled it right) tricorder

14 If you could bring anything back from extinction, what would it be? UK STEM Education

15 Your favorite mode of transport is … Walking

16 What future invention would you like to make (or witness)? Teleportation

17 Ready, Aim, Fire, or Ready, Fire, Aim? FIRE!

18 If you could ask one question of anybody, what would it be and to whom? Failed to think of a question to anyone. I guess knowing a single answer isn't worthwhile

19 When were you happiest? Pretty happy most of the time, especially when being creative

20 What makes you angry? Nothing — I get most annoyed by stupidity

21 What does love feel like? Cuddly

22 Bitcoin or dollars? Gold ingots

23 How much is enough? Too much is never enough

24 What is your greatest achievement? Surviving

25 Beach or adventure holiday? Adventure or something with photographic opportunity

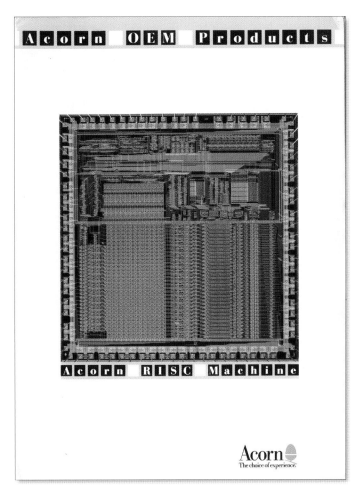

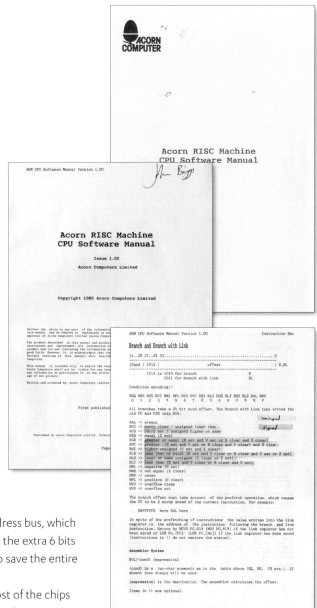

a 32-bit data bus and a 32-bit instructions set but only 26-bit-wide address bus, which was sufficient for the size of computer Acorn required. It also allowed the extra 6 bits to be used to store the processor state allowing a single instruction to save the entire machine state in a single 32-bit word.

Acorn was making computers for the consumer market, so the cost of the chips was vital — hence the 26-bit decision. There was also a requirement for low power, but only because the chip could use a cheap plastic package rather than an expensive ceramic one. As it turned out, the chip was extremely efficient with low power requirement, and proved to be a big step forward for processors.

Acorn had grown dramatically in the two years since the launch of the BBC Micro in 1981, from 30 staff to over 300. In that time the company had moved to new premises, taking over the old Water Pumping Station in Cherry Hinton, and had also commissioned a brand new building on the site — the Silver Building. The Advanced Research and Development (AR&D) team had been created and grew to include Sophie, Steve and what became the founding team of ARM: Al Thomas, who was being mentored by Steve as the next CPU system architect, chip designers Tudor Brown and Mike Muller, and the VLSI team, who took the designs and turned them into real chips, which was led by Robert Heaton (who departed before ARM was formed). There was also Jamie Urquhart, Harry Oldham, Dave Howard, John Biggs, compiler specialists Lee Smith, Harry Meekings and Andy Merritt, algorithms guru David Seal, and Pete Harrod on floating point.

LEFT   The first brochure announcing the release of ARM1, 1985.

RIGHT   The original ARM software manual, 1985.

computer software for all the family

ABOVE A flyer for the BBC Micro, the computer used to design the first ARM chip set.

From a very early stage it was clear that to build the low-cost computer Acorn needed to design not just a RISC processor but a complete system. The high-level system architecture was developed and the system partitioned into four chips: the CPU, a memory controller (MEMC) designed by Steve, a video processor (VIDC) designed by Tudor, and an IO controller (IOC) designed by Mike. The original design envisioned four 68-pin packages, but it soon became clear that to achieve the performance required the CPU would need 84 pins, and the system architecture was set.

Sophie finished the definition of the ARM1 instruction set in December 1983, and handed it over to Steve. Through 1984 he developed the reference model for the microarchitecture — how the instructions would be implemented — using models written in the BASIC programming language and running on the BBC Micro. It was then given to the VLSI team to implement the design and test it against the models.

The design of the processor was tested and completed, with the "tapeout" ready in January 1985. The computer tape was delivered by hand to VLSI Technology's European headquarters in a very cold and snowy Munich. The full design used just 25,000 transistors and was built in a 3-micron process (where the smallest feature of the transistor, the gate, measured 3 microns). This was a tiny fraction of, say, Motorola's 32-bit 68020. Launched in 1984 and used in the Apple Macintosh and Lisa computers, the Motorola chip had 250,000 transistors built in a 2-micron process.

The ARM1 began what came to be a key tradition for the engineers at ARM: when the first chip was returned from VLSI's fab, Acorn co-founder Hermann Hauser opened a bottle of champagne. That's why there are lots of empty champagne bottles scattered around the company HQ — they're all historic icons, mementos of the creation of past chips.

ARM1

DATE April 26, 1985

TECHNOLOGY VLSI "CMOSD2A" 3.0 µm (2-layer metal)

TRANSISTORS 25K

SIZE 50 mm²

FREQUENCY 6 MHz

POWER 120 mW

ARCHITECTURE ARMv1

µARCHITECTURE 3-stage pipeline

DESCRIPTION First ARM silicon

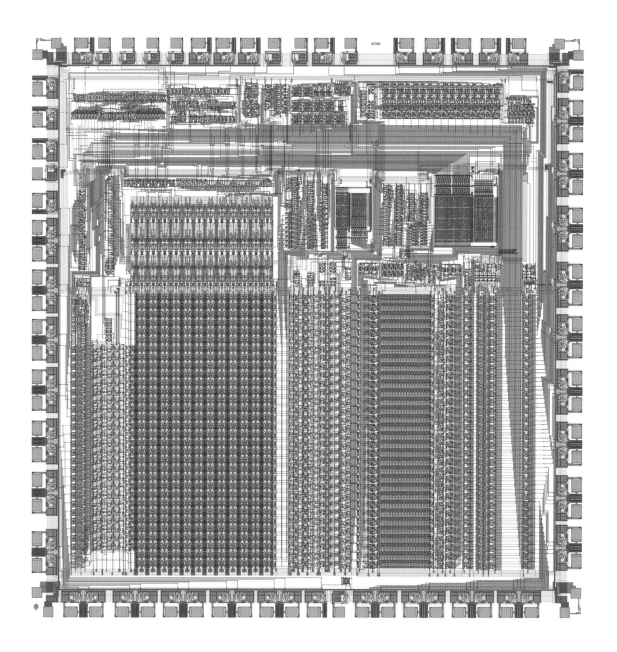

25 × 25 Tudor Brown

YEAR OF BIRTH   1958

COUNTRY OF BIRTH   Wales

CITY OF RESIDENCE   Cambridge

UNIVERSITY + DEGREE
Cambridge, MA Electrical Sciences

TENURE AT ARM   1983-2012

1 **Who or what did you want to be when you grew up?**   Maths teacher

2 **What or who was your first obsession?**   Meccano

3 **Who was your childhood hero (or is now)?**   My Dad

4 **What's your secret?**   Not telling!

5 *Star Trek* or *Star Wars*?   Neither

6 **Did any book change your life? If so, what was it?**   Not that I can remember

7 **Favorite movie:**   *Plenty* (1985)

8 **If you could hear only one piece of music again, what would it be?**   Beethoven's 3rd Symphony

9 **Vinyl, cassette, 8-track, CD, MP3, or streaming?**   CD

10 **What do you prefer: Skype conference call or face-to-face meeting?**   Face-to-face

11 **Your favorite ARM product is:**   iPhone (sorry, boring I know)

12 **The best use of an ARM product is:**   Telling the time

13 **The best use of an ARM product would be …**   Video calling that actually works on low signal

14 **If you could bring anything back from extinction, what would it be?**   Dodo

15 **Your favorite mode of transport is …**   Car

16 **What future invention would you like to make (or witness)?**   Instant transport

17 **Ready, Aim, Fire, or Ready, Fire, Aim?**   Ready Fire Aim Oops

18 **If you could ask one question of anybody, what would it be and to who?**   Jesus: 'Why?'

19 **When were you happiest?**   1990s

20 **What makes you angry?**   Poorly designed products

21 **What does love feel like?**   Contentment

22 **Bitcoin or dollars?**   Dollars

23 **How much is enough?**   Never

24 **What is your greatest achievement?**   Cutting my car radio in half

25 **Beach or adventure holiday?**   Adventure

The ARM1 was developed and shipped as a £4,000 add-on board to the BBC B Micro, to act as a development system. Unknown to the creators, one of the purchasers of their development system was a team of engineers in California, working at Apple.

As it turned out, the chip proved to be incredibly low powered. The target was for under 1 W so that it would go into low-cost plastic packaging. But there was a problem with the power supply to the first version, which meant that there was no power to the chip at all — and yet it was running. It turned out that the current was coming from the inputs to the chip rather than from the power supply, and leaking out to power the rest of the device. That accounted for the unexplained crashes when all the inputs went to zero — there was no power available. Sophie and Steve determined that the whole chip was running on about a tenth of a watt (120 mW).

However, Acorn was going through turmoil at the time. The Electron home computer had missed the lucrative Christmas market of 1983 becaseu they couldn't manufacture enough in time. And by early 1984, their warehouse was filling up with unsold stock. That was because the home computer market was collapsing, and other home computers such as the Dragon 32 and 64, the Amiga and the Commodore 64 were also struggling to sell enough to keep their manufacturers in business.

The economic downturn in the PC business hit Acorn — with its high overheads and staff costs — hard. It turned to Italian typewriter and computer-maker Olivetti for

BELOW In 1984 Apple launched the $10,000 Lisa home computer. The Project A team were one of the first customers in the UK, eager to see what the competition were producing.

help, and in the middle of 1985 the Italian company bought a 49 percent stake. The deal led to changes in management, and proved an important part in the story of ARM.

In an innovative move (at least for the UK), founder Hermann Hauser, when setting up Acorn, had given all the engineers share options in the company. By the time of the Olivetti rescue the value of these shares had collapsed, to the point where they were worth, according to one engineer, the price of a curry.

All the while during the Olivetti talks no mention had been made of the Acorn RISC chip design team, possibly because Olivetti made PC clones using Intel's x86 processors. Whatever the reason, it proved crucial in the founding of ARM.

Among the changes made at Acorn in 1985, Robert Heaton moved to the US to take up the role of director of engineering for US2, the US operation of the newly launched European Silicon Structures (ES2). It was Europe's answer to ASIC companies like VLSI Technology and LSI Logic, and employed Robin Saxby as UK managing director. It had been backed by $5 million from venture capital firm Advent and $60 million from Olivetti, Saab, British Aerospace and Philips. So US2 was a significant venture, intended to compete on equal terms with the US. But it used a different technology — instead of a metal mask on top of a gate array, ES2 was using a technology developed in Europe that used an electron beam to write the metal layer on top. This promised to be fast and efficient, but ultimately proved to be much slower than the more traditional approach. (Four decades later e-beam technology may prove to be the technology that maintains Moore's Law at 7 nanometers and below.)

BELOW The A500 second processor, the first development board for the complete chip set.

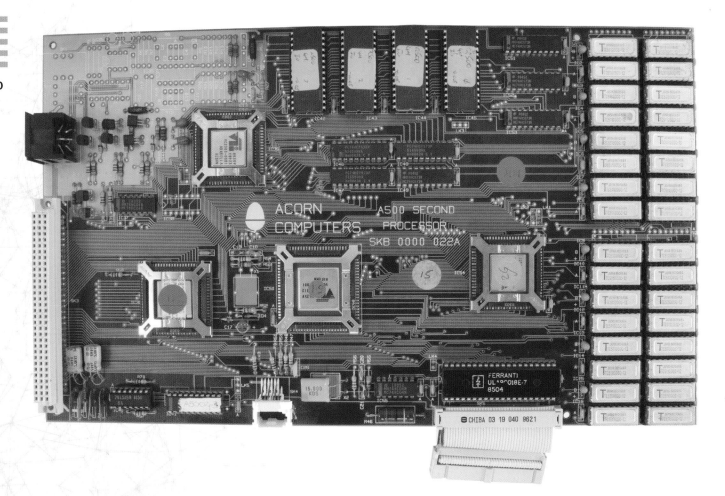

VIDC

DATE 11 p.m., October 22, 1985

TECHNOLOGY VLSI "CMN25G" 2.4 μm (2-layer metal)

TRANSISTORS 18,039

SIZE 5.35 x 5.77 mm

FREQUENCY 10 MHz

DESCRIPTION Video controller for Acorn Archimedes

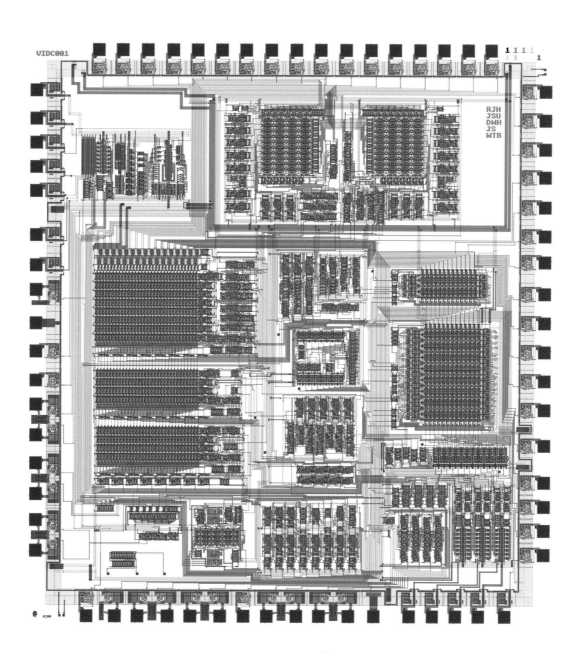

IOC

DATE 4:30 p.m., April 30, 1986
TECHNOLOGY VLSI "CMN20G" 2.0 μm (2-layer metal)
TRANSISTORS 11,130
SIZE 4.61 x 4.62 mm
FREQUENCY 8-10 MHz
DESCRIPTION Input/output controller for Acorn Archimedes

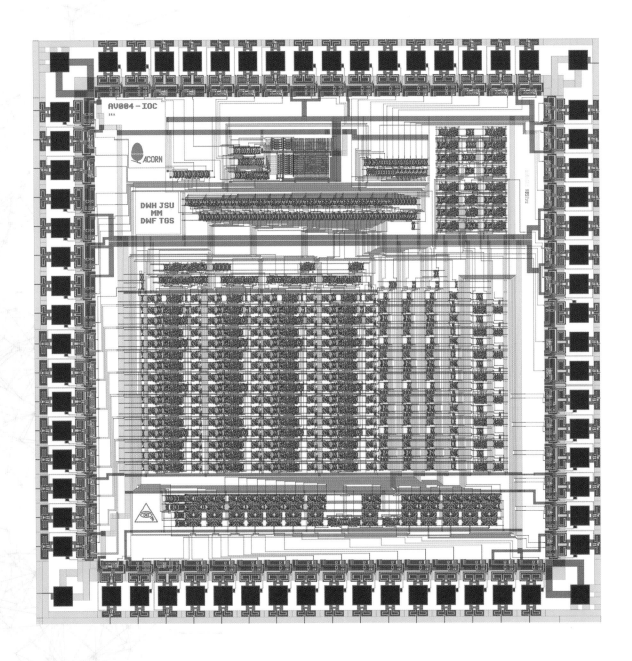

MEMC

DATE	8 p.m., February 26, 1986
TECHNOLOGY	VLSI "CMN20G" 2.0 μm (2-layer metal)
TRANSISTORS	29,530
SIZE	5.60 x 5.52 mm
FREQUENCY	12 MHz
DESCRIPTION	Memory controller for Acorn Archimedes

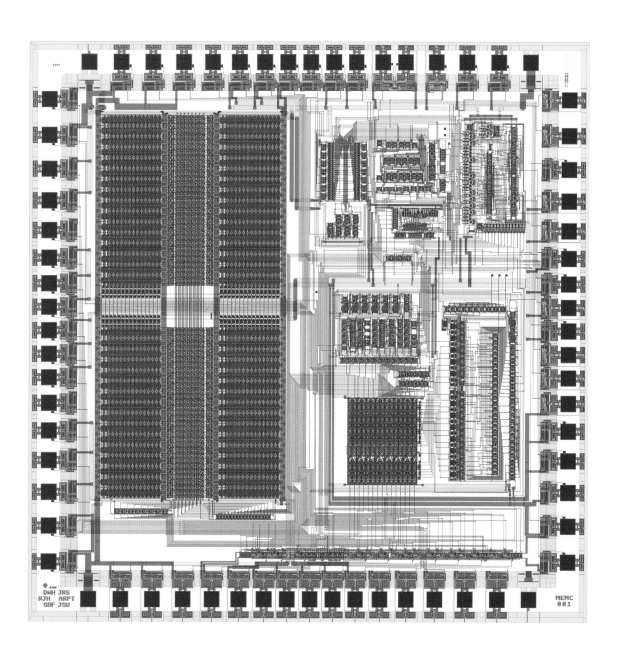

In 1985 the US PC market was also suffering a downturn. Xerox's Palo Alto Research Center, where many computer innovations from windowed software to the mouse were conceived, reduced its headcount. Hermann Hauser took advantage of this by setting up the Acorn Palo Alto Research Lab in order to develop an operating system for this exciting new chip architecture. He recruited Jim Mitchell to be director of engineering, based in the US, with Steve Furber as the de facto manager of AR&D on the ground in Cambridge.

The ARM2, delivered in 1987 on a 2-micron process by VLSI, coupled with MEMC, VIDC and IOC, formed the heart of a new product line for Acorn: the Archimedes RISC PC. At the same time a new approach to making chips was emerging. In 1984 Morris Chang moved from being chief operating officer of chip giant Texas Instruments to General Instrument. In that turbulent year of 1985 he was encouraged by the Taiwanese government to look at how Taiwan could be a significant player in the emerging electronics market, and left GI to become the president of the Industrial Technology Research Institute in that country. His approach was to offer foundry services, taking the tapes and producing the chips in volume, but not to undertake the design of the chips themselves. Like the ARM business model, this allowed their customers to innovate on top of a shared platform. This new "fabless" model was driven by the changing capital costs of chipmaking. In 1990 the cost of a chip fabrication plant, or fab, was between $200 million and $500 million. By 2000 it was $1 billion, and by 2010 around $5 billion. In 2015 Samsung spent more than $14 billion on a new fab.

BELOW Mike Muller in his paperless office, showing off the A500 (1987), the pre-production protoype for the Archimedes family.

ACORN
HIGH PERFORMANCE COMPUTER SYSTEMS

Archimedes 440

Acorn
The choice of experience.

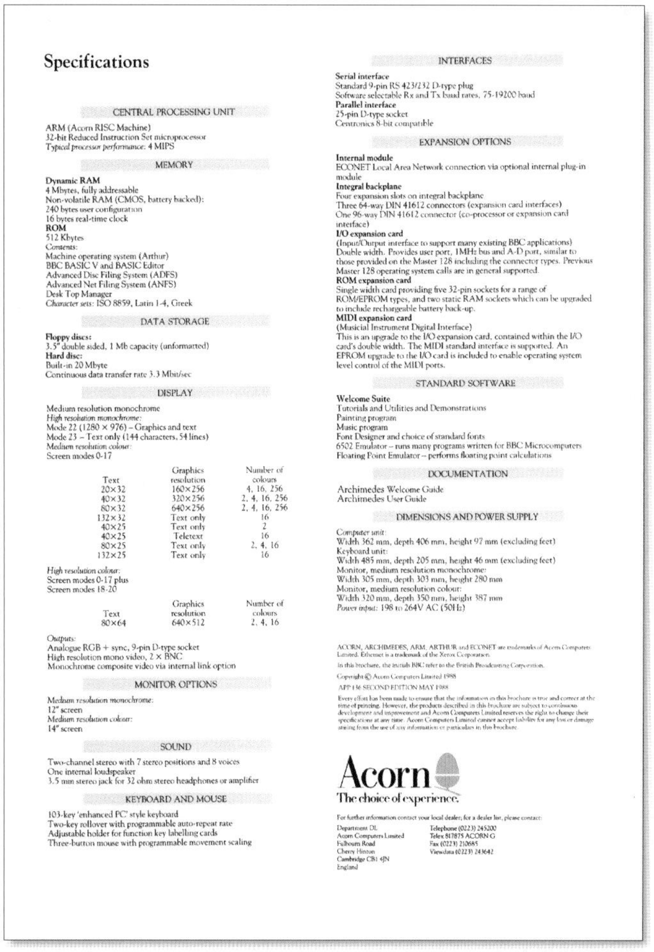

Specifications

CENTRAL PROCESSING UNIT

ARM (Acorn RISC Machine)
32-bit Reduced Instruction Set microprocessor
Typical processor performance: 4 MIPS

MEMORY

Dynamic RAM
4 Mbytes, fully addressable
Non-volatile RAM (CMOS, battery backed):
240 bytes user configuration
16 bytes real-time clock
ROM
512 Kbytes
Contents:
Machine operating system (Arthur)
BBC BASIC V and BASIC Editor
Advanced Disc Filing System (ADFS)
Advanced Net Filing System (ANFS)
Desk Top Manager
Character sets: ISO 8859, Latin 1-4, Greek

DATA STORAGE

Floppy discs:
3.5" double sided, 1 Mb capacity (unformatted)
Hard disc:
Built-in 20 Mbyte
Continuous data transfer rate 3.3 Mbit/sec

DISPLAY

Medium resolution monochrome
High resolution monochrome:
Mode 22 (1280 × 976) – Graphics and text
Mode 23 – Text only (144 characters, 54 lines)
Medium resolution colour:
Screen modes 0-17

Text	Graphics resolution	Number of colours
20×32	160×256	4, 16, 256
40×32	320×256	2, 4, 16, 256
80×32	640×256	2, 4, 16, 256
132×32	Text only	16
40×25	Text only	2
40×25	Teletext	16
80×25	Text only	2, 4, 16
132×25	Text only	16

High resolution colour:
Screen modes 0-17 plus
Screen modes 18-20

Text	Graphics resolution	Number of colours
80×64	640×512	2, 4, 16

Outputs:
Analogue RGB + sync, 9-pin D-type socket
High resolution mono video, 2 × BNC
Monochrome composite video via internal link option

MONITOR OPTIONS

Medium resolution monochrome:
12" screen
Medium resolution colour:
14" screen

SOUND

Two-channel stereo with 7 stereo positions and 8 voices
One internal loudspeaker
3.5 mm stereo jack for 32 ohm stereo headphones or amplifier

KEYBOARD AND MOUSE

103-key 'enhanced PC' style keyboard
Two-key rollover with programmable auto-repeat rate
Adjustable holder for function key labelling cards
Three-button mouse with programmable movement scaling

INTERFACES

Serial interface
Standard 9-pin RS 423/232 D-type plug
Software selectable Rx and Tx baud rates, 75-19200 baud
Parallel interface
25-pin D-type socket
Centronics 8-bit compatible

EXPANSION OPTIONS

Internal module
ECONET Local Area Network connection via optional internal plug-in module
Integral backplane
Four expansion slots on integral backplane
Three 64-way DIN 41612 connectors (expansion card interfaces)
One 96-way DIN 41612 connector (co-processor or expansion card interface)
I/O expansion card
(Input/Output interface to support many existing BBC applications)
Double width. Provides user port, 1MHz bus and A-D port, similar to those provided on the Master 128 including the connector types. Previous Master 128 operating system calls are in general supported.
ROM expansion card
Single width card providing five 32-pin sockets for a range of ROM/EPROM types, and two static RAM sockets which can be upgraded to include rechargeable battery back-up.
MIDI expansion card
(Musicial Instrument Digital Interface)
This is an upgrade to the I/O expansion card, contained within the I/O card's double width. The MIDI standard interface is supported. An EPROM upgrade to the I/O card is included to enable operating system level control of the MIDI ports.

STANDARD SOFTWARE

Welcome Suite
Tutorials and Utilities and Demonstrations
Painting program
Music program
Font Designer and choice of standard fonts
6502 Emulator – runs many programs written for BBC Microcomputers
Floating Point Emulator – performs floating point calculations

DOCUMENTATION

Archimedes Welcome Guide
Archimedes User Guide

DIMENSIONS AND POWER SUPPLY

Computer unit:
Width 362 mm, depth 406 mm, height 97 mm (excluding feet)
Keyboard unit:
Width 485 mm, depth 205 mm, height 46 mm (excluding feet)
Monitor, medium resolution monochrome:
Width 305 mm, depth 303 mm, height 280 mm
Monitor, medium resolution colour:
Width 320 mm, depth 350 mm, height 387 mm
Power input: 198 to 264V AC (50Hz)

ACORN, ARCHIMEDES, ARM, ARTHUR and ECONET are trademarks of Acorn Computers Limited. Ethernet is a trademark of the Xerox Corporation.

In this brochure, the initials BBC refer to the British Broadcasting Corporation.

Copyright © Acorn Computers Limited 1988

APP 136 SECOND EDITION MAY 1988

Every effort has been made to ensure that the information in this brochure is true and correct at the time of printing. However, the products described in this brochure are subject to continuous development and improvement and Acorn Computers Limited reserves the right to change their specifications at any time. Acorn Computers Limited cannot accept liability for any loss or damage arising from the use of any information or particulars in this brochure.

Acorn
The choice of experience.

For further information contact your local dealer; for a dealer list, please contact:

Department DL
Acorn Computers Limited
Fulbourn Road
Cherry Hinton
Cambridge CB1 4JN
England

Telephone (0223) 245200
Telex 817875 ACORN G
Fax (0223) 210685
Viewdata (0223) 243642

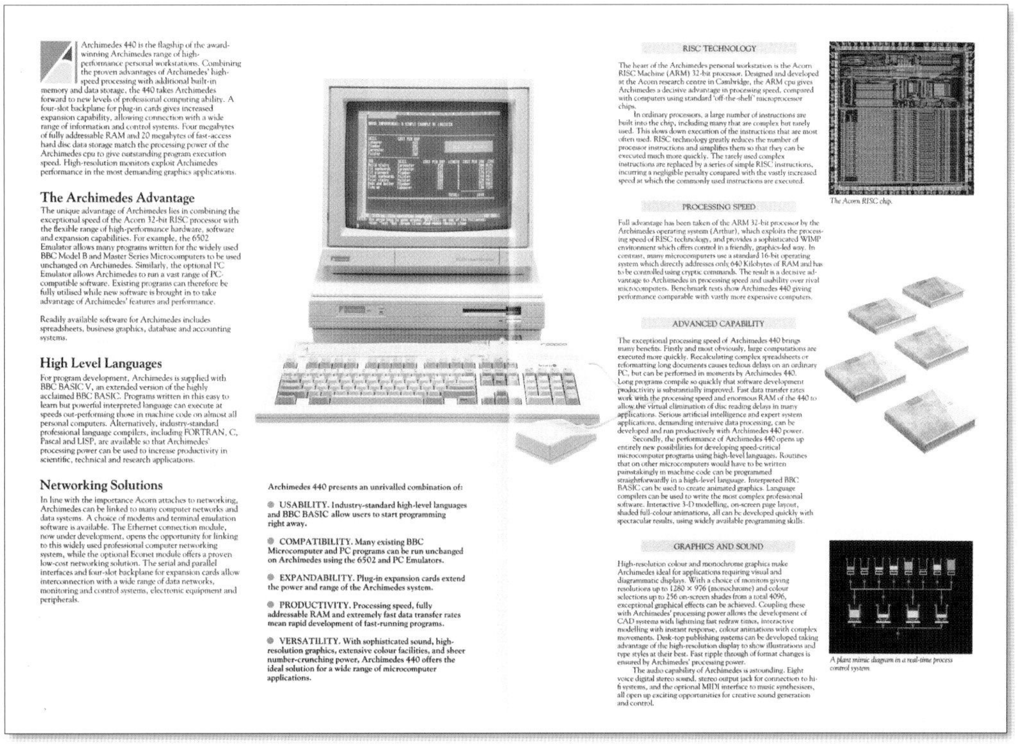

Archimedes 440 is the flagship of the award-winning Archimedes range of high-performance personal workstations. Combining the proven advantages of Archimedes' high-speed processing with additional built-in memory and data storage, the 440 takes Archimedes forward to new levels of professional computing ability. A four-slot backplane for plug-in cards gives increased expansion capability, allowing connection with a wide range of information and control systems. Four megabytes of fully addressable RAM and 20 megabytes of fast-access hard disc data storage match the processing power of the Archimedes cpu to give outstanding program execution speed. High-resolution monitors exploit Archimedes performance in the most demanding graphics applications.

The Archimedes Advantage

The unique advantage of Archimedes lies in combining the exceptional speed of the Acorn 32-bit RISC processor with the flexible range of high-performance hardware, software and expansion capabilities. For example, the 6502 Emulator allows many programs written for the widely used BBC Model B and Master Series Microcomputers to be used unchanged on Archimedes. Similarly, the optional PC Emulator allows Archimedes to run a vast range of PC-compatible software. Existing programs can therefore be fully utilised while new software is brought in to take advantage of Archimedes' features and performance.

Readily available software for Archimedes includes spreadsheets, business graphics, database and accounting systems.

High Level Languages

For program development, Archimedes is supplied with BBC BASIC V, an extended version of the highly acclaimed BBC BASIC. Programs written in this easy to learn but powerful interpreted language can execute at speeds out-performing those in machine code on almost all personal computers. Alternatively, industry-standard professional language compilers, including FORTRAN, C, Pascal and LISP, are available so that Archimedes' processing power can be used to increase productivity in scientific, technical and research applications.

Networking Solutions

In line with the importance Acorn attaches to networking, Archimedes can be linked to many computer networks and data systems. A choice of modems and terminal emulation software is available. The Ethernet connection module, now under development, opens the opportunity for linking to this widely used professional computer networking system, while the optional Econet module offers a proven low-cost networking solution. The serial and parallel interfaces and four-slot backplane for expansion cards allow interconnection with a wide range of data networks, monitoring and control systems, electronic equipment and peripherals.

Archimedes 440 presents an unrivalled combination of:

- **USABILITY. Industry-standard high-level languages and BBC BASIC allow users to start programming right away.**
- **COMPATIBILITY. Many existing BBC Microcomputer and PC programs can be run unchanged on Archimedes using the 6502 and PC Emulators.**
- **EXPANDABILITY. Plug-in expansion cards extend the power and range of the Archimedes system.**
- **PRODUCTIVITY. Processing speed, fully addressable RAM and extremely fast data transfer rates mean rapid development of fast-running programs.**
- **VERSATILITY. With sophisticated sound, high-resolution graphics, extensive colour facilities, and sheer number-crunching power, Archimedes 440 offers the ideal solution for a wide range of microcomputer applications.**

RISC TECHNOLOGY

The heart of the Archimedes personal workstation is the Acorn RISC Machine (ARM) 32-bit processor. Designed and developed at the Acorn research centre in Cambridge, the ARM cpu gives Archimedes a decisive advantage in processing speed, compared with computers using standard 'off-the-shelf' microprocessor chips.

In ordinary processors, a large number of instructions are built into the chip, including many that are complex but rarely used. This slows down execution of the instructions that are most often used. RISC technology greatly reduces the number of processor instructions and simplifies them so that they can be executed much more quickly. The rarely used complex instructions are replaced by a series of simple RISC instructions, incurring a negligible penalty compared with the vastly increased speed at which the commonly used instructions are executed.

The Acorn RISC chip.

PROCESSING SPEED

Full advantage has been taken of the ARM 32-bit processor by the Archimedes operating system (Arthur), which exploits the processing speed of RISC technology, and provides a sophisticated WIMP environment which offers control in a friendly, graphics-led way. In contrast, many microcomputers use a standard 16-bit operating system which directly addresses only 640 Kilobytes of RAM and has to be controlled using cryptic commands. The result is a decisive advantage to Archimedes in processing speed and usability over rival microcomputers. Benchmark tests show Archimedes 440 giving performance comparable with vastly more expensive computers.

ADVANCED CAPABILITY

The exceptional processing speed of Archimedes 440 brings many benefits. Firstly and most obviously, large computations are executed more quickly. Recalculating complex spreadsheets or reformatting long documents causes tedious delays on an ordinary PC, but can be performed in moments by Archimedes 440. Long programs compile so quickly that software development productivity is substantially improved. Fast data transfer rates work with the processing speed and enormous RAM of the 440 to allow the virtual elimination of disc reading delays in many applications. Serious artificial intelligence and expert system applications, demanding intensive data processing, can be developed and run productively with Archimedes 440 power.

Secondly, the performance of Archimedes 440 opens up entirely new possibilities for developing speed-critical microcomputer programs using high-level languages. Routines that on other microcomputers would have to be written painstakingly in machine code can be programmed straightforwardly in a high-level language. Interpreted BBC BASIC can be used to create animated graphics. Language compilers can be used to write the most complex professional software. Interactive 3-D modelling, on-screen page layout, shaded full-colour animations, all can be developed quickly with spectacular results, using widely available programming skills.

GRAPHICS AND SOUND

High-resolution colour and monochrome graphics make Archimedes ideal for applications requiring visual and diagrammatic displays. With a choice of monitors giving resolutions up to 1280 × 976 (monochrome) and colour selections up to 256 on-screen shades from a total 4096, exceptional graphical effects can be achieved. Coupling these with Archimedes' processing power allows the development of CAD systems with lightning fast redraw times, interactive modelling with instant response, colour animations with complex movements. Desk-top publishing systems can be developed taking advantage of the high-resolution display to show illustrations and type styles at their best. Fast ripple through of format changes is ensured by Archimedes' processing power.

The audio capability of Archimedes is astounding. Eight voice digital stereo sound, stereo output jack for connection to hi-fi systems, and the optional MIDI interface to music synthesisers, all open up exciting opportunities for creative sound generation and control.

A plant mimic diagram in a real-time process control system

LEFT Sales brochure for the Archimedes 400 system.

RIGHT Acorn User was profiling the story of Acorn computers, just as the end was in sight.

Chang saw there was a new opportunity. Companies could design their own chips and they didn't need to have their own fabs. This significantly lowered the barriers to entry for new companies, and it spurred a new wave of innovation, creating a new breed of "fabless" chip companies. It also drove the emerging electronic design automation (EDA) tools companies, and the development of high performance computers, or workstations. In 1982, Sun Microsystems began building workstations, and by 1985 was developing the SPARC processor that used the same RISC technique as ARM. There was no shortage of companies looking to develop their own chips, and in time even the established chip companies with their own fabs began to use external foundries for their production..

All of these factors convinced Chang and his commercial backer Philips to invest in fabs in the Science Park at Hsinchu in 1987 and to create Taiwan Semiconductor Manufacturing Company — who would become a key partner of ARM.

Despite significant investment in the brand new object-oriented operating system (ARX) written in Modular-2+, led by Jim and the team in Palo Alto, it became obvious that it would never be ready in time for the planned launch — in June 1987 — of the Archimedes RISC PC. For the time, the hardware was impressive, with an 8 MHz ARM2 microprocessor, color displays and integrated stereo audio. The basic model, the Archimedes 310, came with 512 KB of memory and an integrated floppy drive for £799 retail. The top of the range A440 boasted 4 MB of memory and an integrated 20 MB hard drive, at an eye-watering £2,299 for a home computer. And the operating system? Well, that was developed in five months, and was initially launched as Arthur, later renamed RISC OS. It was written mainly in assembly language and was hard coded into 512 KB of ROM, so no bugs were allowed.

As the Archimedes 300 and 400 began hitting the streets, the team turned its attention to improved versions of the chip set, producing ARM3, MEMC1a and VIDC1a and extending the architecture to ARMv2 by adding two SWAP instructions in an attempt to improve the performance of ARX. The ARX project would continue for another year or so until it became clear that it would never deliver, and the design center was closed.

A move to a 1.5-micron process gave more space on ARM3, still using the ARMv2 architecture, enabling a 4KB cache memory to be added to further speed up the performance. But all had not gone well at Acorn since Olivetti had taken overall control. Hermann Hauser left the board of Acorn in 1988 to set up a new venture, the Active Book Company. He planned to develop a portable computer, using a new version of the ARM processor where the clock could be scaled right back to zero to save power. This would be the fully static ARM2aS.

Malcolm Bird joined Acorn as director of engineering in November 1989 from PA Consulting, also in Cambridge. Acorn had a reputation for being technically innovative,

LEFT   The ARM3 design team (l-r): Al Thomas, Jamie Urquhart, Dave Howard and Harry Oldham, in the silver building.

RIGHT   In *Back to the Future II* (1989) Marty McFly visited June 2015, where the world was uncannily accurately shown, with flat-screen TVs, a kind of Skype and tablet computers in everyday use. All we need now are hoverboards.

if commercially unsuccessful. After six years with PA, advising people what to do, he thought it would be nice to go back to working in technology.

In Cambridge, one of Malcolm's first moves was to disband Steve's AR&D group and put the engineers back among the technical group, spreading responsibility between the two teams. The combined team was then focused on the ARM3 for the Archimedes A540, which used the existing Archimedes 300 and 400 cases and boards, while the design went ahead with the next-generation A5000 machine. The A540

25 × 25 Andy Merritt

1 Who or what did you want to be when you grew up? I had no idea at all, so software engineering just happened by default!

2 What or who was your first obsession? Toyah Wilcox — heck, I was a fresh-faced teenager and it was the early '80s ...

3 Who was your childhood hero (or is now)? I don't really do heroes, as they are all flawed when you look closely.

4 What's your secret? No truth or dare here, so I'll interpret this as meaning 'secret to success' or some such: I remember Robin Saxby always saying 'Work hard and play hard'. I liked this a lot (and still do). I always keep busy and get lots done whatever I am doing, and similarly with my free time I make sure I get to do lots of fun stuff. Perhaps it could also be summed up 'no rest for the wicked'?

5 *Star Trek* or *Star Wars*? *Trek*. But not the original, only TNG onwards.

6 Did any book change your life? If so, what was it? *The Lord of the Rings* (1954), J. R. R. Tolkien. I remember reading it at about the age of 10 and being utterly transfixed. Not sure how it has changed my life exactly, but it has changed my daughter's as we named her Tinuviel.

7 Favorite movie: Well, from the above you'll guess I like the *Lord of the Rings* trilogy (2001-2003) a lot. Other than that I'll pick *The Matrix* (1999).

8 If you could hear only one piece of music again, what would it be? I listen to too much music to select just one thing, so instead I'll tell you what I'm listening to right now: Tarja's *Victim of Ritual* (2013).

9 Vinyl, cassette, 8-track, CD, MP3, or streaming? MP3 simply for the convenience and transportability. I still use CDs a lot, and still even have a turntable set up, though only to record stuff from my aging vinyl collection...

10 What do you prefer: Skype conference call or face-to-face meeting? Face-to-face — 100 percent

11 Your favorite ARM product is: Psion 5MX. Anyone who knows me, knows that I still have one with me all the time!!!

12 The best use of an ARM product is: (see above)

13 The best use of an ARM product would be ... Sorry, Master, my Fu is weak. I've been out of the industry too long now to give sensible answers. Sorry.

14 If you could bring anything back from extinction, what would it be? Never thought about it ... How about Kurt Cobain?

15 Your favorite mode of transport is ... Telekinesis. Not having developed that, I use a bicycle.

16 What future invention would you like to make (or witness)? FTL Spaceships. Let's get humanity off this one lump of rock!

17 Ready, Aim, Fire, or Ready, Fire, Aim? Sorry, I haven't a clue what you mean!

18 If you could ask one question of anybody, what would it be and to whom? I'd ask God what it's all really supposed to be about!

19 When were you happiest? No one time, and amazingly I'm still happy even these days now and then. I do recall times I spent in Nepal in 2002-2003 very fondly, but then I nearly died there, too. For me life needs highs and lows — if you don't have the lows you won't notice the highs!

20 What makes you angry? Greedy, selfish, inconsiderate, intolerant people. Sadly that means most of us at some time or another.

21 What does love feel like? Pretty damn good!

22 Bitcoin or dollars? Dollars.

23 How much is enough? Enough is only as much as you need. Greed is as much as you want. Wisdom is only wanting what you need.

24 What is your greatest achievement? I have never aimed to achieve anything great, just try to do lots of small things as best I can.

25 Beach or adventure holiday? Adventure holiday no question. Lying on a beach is just boring.

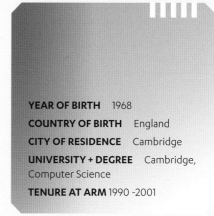

YEAR OF BIRTH 1968
COUNTRY OF BIRTH England
CITY OF RESIDENCE Cambridge
UNIVERSITY + DEGREE Cambridge, Computer Science
TENURE AT ARM 1990 -2001

would use additional MEMC memory controllers. Although a single MEMC could only handle 4 MB of memory it could be put together with three others to support 16 MB of memory, which (for that time) was a massive achievement. This would also allow for a more complex operating system, Arthur 2, to become the RISC OS.

The ARM chip set had been designed by Acorn for Acorn, with VLSI Technology as a contract manufacturer. But Acorn had little experience of manufacturing chips in volume, so in exchange for VLSI Technology providing resources and expertise to develop the test infrastructure to bring the original chip set to volume, VLSI was granted a license to sell the chips on the open market to its customers, and became the first ARM licensee. This was the beginning of the ARM IP business model.

Ever since the crises of 1985, the idea to spin out the chip design group had sporadically been explored at Acorn. There was even a file marked Newco (for new company) in the desk Malcolm inherited from Jim Mitchell.

With the Olivetti connection, Malcolm approached French chip company Thomson-CSF, which later merged with SGS to become STMicroelectronics. His proposals included combining design teams or joint chip development, but they came to nothing. He also talked to VLSI Technology, while they were making ARM chips, but it soon became clear that the chief executive Al Stein wasn't going to put in any money.

Meanwhile, Steve had decided to leave Acorn in order to take up the chair of computer engineering at the university in his home city, Manchester. He took with him a wealth of expertise on the ARM architecture that would be relevant for the next 20 years and more.

Apple had been evaluating the ARM development system as one of the options for a revolutionary handheld computer it was developing in a separate, skunkworks project (the Newton). But it had initially chosen a processor from AT&T called the Hobbit, which had been developed at AT&T's world-famous Bell Labs. While there had been lots of razzamatazz around the launch of the Hobbit, the reality of delivering working chips proved to be problematic. (In an ironic twist, Hermann's Active Book Company was bought by AT&T in July 1991 and merged with its EO subsidiary, and the

RIGHT Larry Tesler, leader of Apple's Newton project, in 1989. He became one of ARM's first non-executive directors.

processor was changed to the Hobbit. The EO Personal Communicator was launched in 1992, but the company closed in 1993.) Larry Tesler and his team evaluated five other chips, talking to Motorola, IBM, AMD and even Intel, as well as MIPS, about low-power processors suitable for portable applications. Everyone was promising the world, of course. If several people like what's on the roadmap, the part gets made. If none do, the roadmap changes and the company denies it ever intended to do anything like that. In the end, "Everyone talked about their roadmaps, everyone had something that would be ready next year, but it came down to Hobbit and ARM, and we went with AT&T's Hobbit," as Larry explained. That was perhaps partly as a result of Acorn being seen as a competitor to Apple in the education market.

When the Hobbit project ran into trouble, Apple needed an alternative. Malcolm recalls that it was Hermann who talked to Larry Tesler, Apple's vice president of research and development at the time, on one of his networking visits to the Valley on behalf of Active Book. "Basically," he pointed out to Larry, "you've always been interested in ARM, you've always been playing with it." Larry said he couldn't see it going anywhere, and besides, it was owned by a competitor, which ruled it out for him. That's when they came up with the idea of the spinout. So Hermann called Malcolm, saying, "This is the plan ..."

Having Apple use the ARM processor (as well as Active Book) would have been a big boost to the plans for forming a new company. Which is what Malcolm Bird wanted

ABOVE   A 1990 trade advert for VLSI, ARM's first semiconductor partner.

25×25 Jamie Urquhart

YEAR OF BIRTH 1957

COUNTRY OF BIRTH UK

CITY OF RESIDENCE somewhere near Cambridge

UNIVERSITY + DEGREE Bath University: Physics and Physical Electronics

TENURE AT ARM From the beginning–2002

1 Who or what did you want to be when you grew up? Train driver, fast jet pilot, astronaut, nuclear physicist, something to do with Electronics ...

2 What or who was your first obsession? Things that go bang ...

3 Who was your childhood hero (or is now)? Pass — never really had one

4 What's your secret? Enjoy what you do, work with fine people and get to know yourself

5 *Star Trek* or *Star Wars*? *Star Trek*

6 Did any book change your life? If so, what was it? *Swallows and Amazons* (1930), Arthur Ransome

7 Favorite movie: *2001: A Space Odyssey* (1968)

8 If you could hear only one piece of music again, what would it be? *Stairway to Heaven* (1971), Led Zeppelin (I have just listened to it twice on being reminded)

9 Vinyl, cassette, 8-track, CD, MP3, or streaming? Streaming

10 What do you prefer: Skype conference call or face-to-face meeting? Horses for courses, but ... if I had to jump off the fence it would be face-to-face

11 Your favorite ARM product is: The first ARM processor ...

12 The best use of an ARM product is: Nokia 6110

13 The best use of an ARM product would be ... World peace

14 If you could bring anything back from extinction, what would it be? I'd settle for keeping the hedgehog from going extinct.

15 Your favorite mode of transport is ... Bicycle

16 What future invention would you like to make (or witness)? Warp drive

17 Ready, Aim, Fire, or Ready, Fire, Aim? RFA

18 If you could ask one question of anybody, what would it be and to whom? 'How's it going?' to an extraterrestrial intelligence. (There is a more personal answer to this question — AI ...)

19 When were you happiest? In the present — whenever it was ...

20 What makes you angry? Dogma

21 What does love feel like? Spring flowers, summer sun, autumn calm, crunchy snow

22 Bitcoin or dollars? Dollars

23 How much is enough? Enough

24 What is your greatest achievement? Discovering Maslow's hierarchy of needs was right from a personal perspective

25 Beach or adventure holiday? Adventure holiday

to achieve when he traveled to the US in early 1990 to see Larry at the Cupertino Inn. There was a huge amount resting on their meeting. Apple's Newton MessagePad was the pet project of John Sculley, the chief executive at the company at the time, and he was desperate to make it work. Having been brought in from Pepsi by Steve Jobs, Sculley had ousted Jobs in a bitter boardroom battle. The Newton was his chance to demonstrate that he could be every bit as successful as Jobs. Which meant a lot rested on the Newton project — and it was having serious problems finding the right chip.

Shortly after the Cupertino meeting, Larry took several engineers from California to Cambridge, in order to quiz the guys at Acorn on their technology. It was a full technical inquisition, and proved that there was serious interest from Apple. If Apple was going to switch processors in the middle of the project, then the decision had to be the right one, and Larry needed a technical assessment. The engineers from Apple met with Mike, Jamie and Tudor, and got on well, delving into the details of the ARM3. All of which was kept very much under wraps. The result of that meeting was that a spin-out from Acorn would soon come into existence — it wouldn't include Sophie because she wanted to remain within Acorn and continue her work on computer systems rather than chips — but it would involve all of the 12 founder members of ARM. ▩

ABOVE   Just before Christmas 1990 the ARM team held a fancy dress party at Lee Smith's house. At least, it looked like fancy dress.

BELOW   Champagne bottles opened to celebrate the successful testing of each of the original ARM chip set (1985-1986).

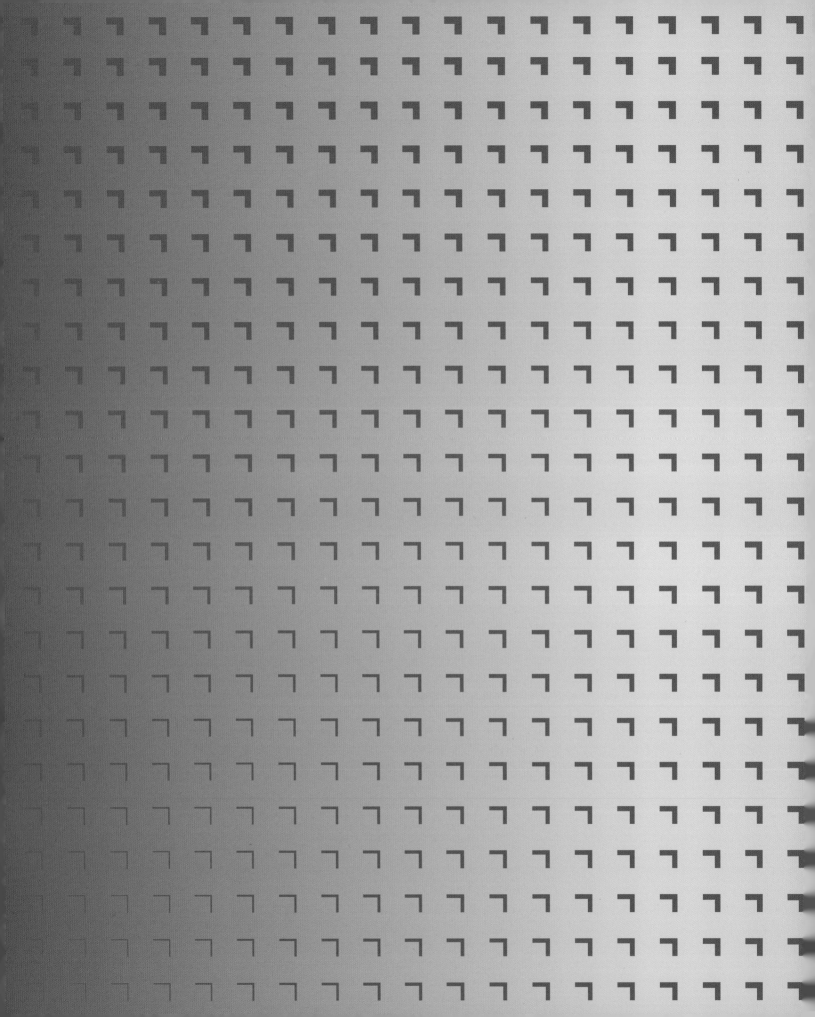

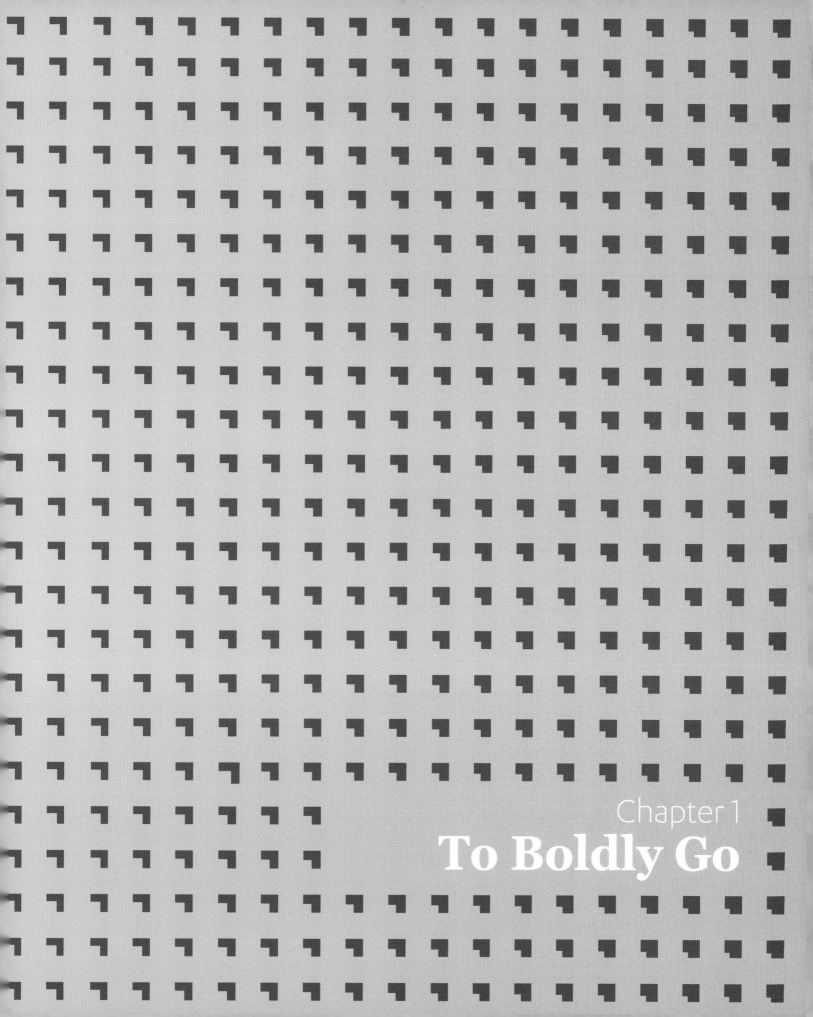

Chapter 1
To Boldly Go

O n a cold November evening in 1990 the mist rolled across bleak fields and curled itself around the country pub. It really was that kind of evening where cars get lost and end up in ditches. And it really was a typical English country pub, with a smoking real fire in the snug and smoky real ale at the bar. It was not the kind of place usually associated with leading-edge technology.

Yet it was the setting for what would prove to be a momentous meeting for the technology industry.

A Saab 9000 pulled up in the car park and two men stepped out. One of them, Robin Saxby, was at a major crossroads in his career, and was hoping the meeting would point him in the right direction. He had been offered a new job, running a startup based in Cambridge, but he needed to know whether it was a sensible move, and for that he needed to meet the team of engineers he would be leading. If he didn't get on with them, or they really didn't like him, then the whole deal was doomed. The other man was Brian O'Donnell, the director of engineering at European Silicon Structures, both men's current employer, and the cheese to Saxby's chalk: quiet, pensive and careful with his words.

In the summer a headhunter had called Robin about the job. It involved working with people who had been spun out of Acorn, a company Robin didn't have much time for, but the new venture also promised the involvement of Apple, which was intriguing.

European Silicon Structures had been the biggest chip startup in Europe in years, but ES2 (as it was known) was struggling. It had expanded into the US, where Saxby had been working. But the recession in the electronics industry at the end of the 1980s meant job cuts and contraction. This was happening to all the big companies — including IBM, VLSI Technology, LSI Logic.

This meeting at the Rose and Crown pub in Ashwell offered him a chance to run what was a potentially world-beating company. This was a very rare opportunity for a UK startup at the end of the 1980s, but it was far from being a sure thing. His experience with the global semiconductor market could be vital to the new company. He had seen how semiconductor companies Motorola, ES2 and US2 operated, and how that could be improved. Plus, he had previously run a smaller venture, Henderson Security.

In assessing the potential move Robin had talked with Robert Heaton before the meeting. Robert, of course, knew both the team and the technology. Robin had some

LEFT   The Space Shuttle Discovery (Mission STS-31) lifts off from Kennedy Space Center, carrying the Hubble Space Telescope in 1990, the year ARM launched.

25 × 25 Harry Oldham

YEAR OF BIRTH   1954

COUNTRY OF BIRTH   UK

CITY OF RESIDENCE   Isle of Wight (rather less population than a city)

UNIVERSITY + DEGREE   Liverpool: BEng + Southampton, PhD

TENURE AT ARM   Joined Acorn 1984. Became ARM 1990 (retired 2007)

1 Who or what did you want to be when you grew up?   A physicist

2 What or who was your first obsession?   Radios

3 Who was your childhood hero (or is now)?   Brunel

4 What's your secret?   Step back and try to keep calm

5 *Star Trek* or *Star Wars*?   *Star Wars*

6 Did any book change your life? If so, what was it?   *The Power of Positive Thinking* (1952), Norman Vincent Peale

7 Favorite movie: *The Man With Two Brains* (1983)

8 If you could hear only one piece of music again, what would it be?   *Adagietto* from Mahler's 5th Symphony (Death in Venice theme)

9 Vinyl, cassette, 8-track, CD, MP3, or streaming?   CD

10 What do you prefer: Skype conference call or face-to-face meeting?   Face-to-face

11 Your favorite ARM product is: ARM7TDMI

12 The best use of an ARM product is: Tablet — Newton, then iPad

13 The best use of an ARM product would be …   Something to help change the world, e.g. health application

14 If you could bring anything back from extinction, what would it be?   Great Auk

15 Your favorite mode of transport is …   Walking

16 What future invention would you like to make (or witness)?   Renewable energy that saves the planet, e.g. fusion

17 Ready, Aim, Fire, or Ready, Fire, Aim?   Ready steady go

18 If you could ask one question of anybody, what would it be and to whom?   Of God — 'Why did you choose to do things this way?'

19 When were you happiest?   On my wedding day

20 What makes you angry?   Slow drivers when I'm in a hurry

21 What does love feel like?   Total peace and joy

22 Bitcoin or dollars?   Dollars. I prefer cash to cards

23 How much is enough?   Nothing in excess

24 What is your greatest achievement?   Having a happy working life and time and health to enjoy my retirement

25 Beach or adventure holiday?   Does a walking holiday count as adventure?

previous experience of Acorn; he had already had a good meeting with Malcolm Bird from Acorn, who'd first identified him as a potential member of the new team, and Apple's Larry Tesler, where they had all bonded over their choice of cars — Saab 9000s. The fact that Saab was an investor in ES2 was an interesting link. Still, Robin was very aware from talking with Robert Heaton that he was the outsider. The team was well established and knew what it wanted to do. Because he was an experienced manager and a salesman, not a chip designer, in order to make a realistic assessment of how good these engineers actually were, he'd asked O'Donnell to come along and quiz them.

Robin was on edge while they waited. A lick of hair that hung down over one eye was constantly being pushed back, and he was continually checking his mobile phone, which was state of the art for the analog models of the day, made by another division of Motorola.

The two chatted quietly over a couple of pints of beer until the door opened and in came a motley group of blokes. One wore sandals, another a workman's jacket. There was nothing to indicate that they were some of the brightest engineers in the world, except they obviously didn't give a damn what other people thought.

"Where the hell have you lot been?" snapped Robin. "Another minute and I'd have left." The group looked surprised. They'd heard he could be hard, but it was a foggy evening, they'd driven for an hour from Cambridge through some nearly deserted countryside, and besides, they'd only said between eight o'clock and nine. They weren't really late, but they were being "Robinned" — something of a chewing out but, if you could take it, it wasn't personal. "I'm never late. It's unprofessional," he continued. For engineers who never really met customers and didn't do meetings like this anyway, it didn't matter. After all, he needed them. They were the designers of some of the most efficient chips on the planet. Without them, there was nothing. The name of their department said it all: Advanced Research and Development.

Some of the group had already encountered Robin, when Malcolm Bird had taken Tudor and Jamie to meet with him at Heathrow airport a week earlier, and they had started to get on well. That meeting had proven to be serendipitous, since Larry Tesler was at Heathrow waiting for a flight back to New York on Concorde and Robin was coming through at the same time on his return from US2 in California.

"One day Malcolm comes in and says we've got this new chief executive we think is quite interested and we'd like you to meet him," recalled Tudor. "He's coming into Heathrow tonight, can you go and meet him?"

Some of the team were not happy with the sudden request, and their responses to it were symptomatic of the resistance Malcolm had been facing from various quarters within AR&D. "Lee wasn't happy with the short notice, but Jamie said he could go, and so we all went down in my car," added Tudor. "We met with Robin, and after an hour Larry went for his plane."

Tudor and Jamie knew when they met him that they could deal with him, and started to work out how the new company would operate. "Jamie and I had a chat with Robin and then Jamie went off to the loo," Tudor recalls, continuing "and Robin asked me if everyone would be happy reporting to Jamie and I said no, I felt it had to be a flatter structure than that."

The Rose & Crown, they told Robin, was roughly halfway between Cambridge, where the engineers were based, and where Robin lived, 70 miles away in Maidenhead, off to the west of London, on the River Thames. Maidenhead was becoming popular with high tech executives for being close to Heathrow airport. Robin had been running US2 while

CONFIDENTIAL

Business Outline for

Advanced RISC Machines Ltd.

This document is copyright and must not be
copied without the prior written consent of
Advanced RISC Machines Ltd.

Issue 0.7   Business Outline   18th March 1991

CONFIDENTIAL

The mission of this company is to:

"Design competitive, high performance, low cost,low power consumption
processors which become the accepted standard in the market they address.

In support of this mission ARM Ltd will develop peripheral cell designs, silicon
design , and software tools and provide design services to third parties."

Issue 0.7   Business Outline

CONFIDENTIAL

11.Manufacturing Strategy

ARM will license or sub-contract the manufacture of its products to Semiconductor partners or fabricators. These Companies will be qualified for prototype, low volume and high volume production. It is well recognised that Foundries today have different strengths, some being excellent for the design phase of a project when fast turn manufacturing and engineering de-bug is required , whilst others are excellent at supplying very high volume.ARM will approve a range of Foundries,Geographically placed in the major markets of Europe, the USA and the Far East.ARM will ensure multi-sourcing capability of its products.

Business Outline   Page 19

CONFIDENTIAL

Business Model for ARM Ltd

	1991	1992	1993	1994	1995
Staff					
Proc dev	4	6	7	7	8
Periph	4	5	5	5	5
Consultancy	2	3	5	5	6
Cust Support	1	1	2	2	2
S/W Support	1	1	1	2	2
Compilers	3	4	4	4	4
Tools	3	4	4	4	4
S & M	2	3	3	3	3
Mgt & Admin	5	6	6	7	7
TOTAL STAFF	25	33	37	39	41
Costs					
Cost/person £k	45	45	45	45	45
Capital £k	500	150	100	100	100
Depreciation £k	100	150	183	117	100
Costed staff £k	1125	1485	1665	1755	1845
Promotion £k	150	150	150	150	150
Expenses £k	300	99	111	117	123
Equpit offset £k	(50)	(100)	(150)	(200)	0
MFG £k	50	101	100	100	100
TOTAL COSTS £k	1675	1884	2059	2039	2318
Revenue					
Royalty/chip %	10.0	10.0	10.0	5.7	5.7
Avg Chip value £	8.7	20.0	20.7	21.1	21.6
Royalty/chip £	0.7	1.3	1.9	0.9	1.1
Chip volume k	335	490	830	1320	1900
Chip Royalty £k	245	648	1544	1140	2000
Cons rate £/yr	120	120	120	120	120
Cons income £k	240	360	600	600	720
License fees £k	250	500	0	500	0
Interest @ 10%	24	11	49	124	
TOTAL REVENUE	761	1519	2193	2364	
Balance					
PBT £k	(914)	(365)	134	325	
PBT/Tot Rev %	(120)	(24)	6	14	
Cum PBT £k	(914)	(1239)	(905)	40	
Investment cash	1750	500	250		
Cash position £k	236	(165)	184	125	
Cum cash £k	236	111	495	1240	

Notes
* All figures at 1990 values

Issue 0.7   Business Outline

Figure 2 shows the embedded control market breakdown. The 32 bit segment where ARM is focusing is growing at 45%.

Figure 2 - Embedded Control Market Breakdown

1989   1995

$198 million

32 bit market $ 1,850 million

☐ 4 bit   ■ 8 bit   ■ 16 bit   ■ 32 bit

Source: Bader Associates Dec 1990

ARM has identified that its major growth areas will be those applications requiring high performance with low cost and power consumption, such as embedded control and DSP (digital signal processing).

Figure 3, next page, shows a pictorial representation of ARM Ltd's business relationships.

What ARM is Seeking :

* licensed semiconductor partners
* licensed design tool partners
* design partners
* investors who will complement, use and enhance ARM technology
* customers requiring the design services of ARM

ARM is seeking capital totalling £4,000,000 from one or more investors.

Advanced RISC Machines Limited   6   Business Plan

ABOVE Pages for the first ARM business plan from March, 1991, including financial projections and an outline of the fabless strategy.

LEFT ARM's first mission statement.

MEMORANDUM   Acorn

To: All Staff   Date: 27 November 1990

From: Sam Wauchope   cc:

Subject: **ADVANCED RISC MACHINES LTD**

Following the earlier meetings when the Directors briefed you all on the possibility of an exciting new
joint venture between ourselves and other parties, I am pleased to confirm that agreements will be signed
this afternoon.

I have attached the official press report on the subject and you will see that the joint venture is between
ourselves, VLSI and Apple Computers, who have come together to form a new company Advanced
RISC Machines Ltd. The company will take, further develop and commercially exploit our ARM
technology. The new and important player is Apple who are investing with us in its further development
so that it can be used in their computing products. (I recommend that you read the Press Release in detail
as it highlights the key benefits for all the partners). The formation of ARM Ltd reaffirms the decision
Acorn and its customers made some years ago on RISC technology. Acorn is still the only company in
the world offering 32-bit RISC technology computers for under £1,000.

This combination in the joint venture is a marvellous opportunity for Acorn to show the world the
performance of our chip and to further exploit our design capabilities. Already about a dozen of our staff
have moved over to work for the new company Advanced RISC Machines Ltd, and they will be
designing ARM 600 (the new name for ARM 4!) which is planned for production next year. ARM
700,800 etc will follow over the next few years, along with updates to the controller designs. This is a
positive investment for us as it ensures the continued development of our unique processor the ARM
chip.

The result is a challenging opportunity for those staff working for ARM Ltd, and equally as important is
the continued challenge to the rest of us to design and develop Acorn Computers that exploit this new
"open" architecture processor to the full.

I know that our two partners in this joint venture share our enthusiasm for its success and I also see it as a
marvellous opportunity for Acorn Computers.

Sam

Sam Wauchope

 News Release

27 November 1990

APPLE COMPUTER UK INVESTS IN RISC LAUNCH

Apple Computer UK Ltd has announced a significant investment in the new
technology company Advanced RISC Machines (ARM).

Apple is taking a 30 % share of ARM, which is being spun off from Acorn Computer.
ARM will attack the growing market for high volume, high performance reduced
instruction set (RISC) computer chips. Other initial shareholders are Acorn Computer
and VLSI.

At a press conference in London, Apple Computer UK managing director Mike Newton
said "We are delighted to be supporting ARM. Apple intends to remain a technological
leader in this extremely competitive industry and build on its reputation as an innovator
in the field of real personal computing. As part of this long term strategy, we currently
invest approximately 8% of our revenues in R&D, and intend to increase this
percentage in coming years. It's also critical to Apple to make a small number of
strategic external investments in strongly differentiated technologies. This
announcement addresses both goals.

"In order to succeed on a global basis in the 1990s and beyond, a company has to be
present in the main poles of economic activity around the world. Apple understood this
necessity early in its existence and established its presence in Europe ten years ago.
Today's announcement marks an expansion of that vision, and an extension of Apple
UK's own investment policy which has funded such projects as Apple Macintosh to ICL
connectivity, Apple to BBC Micro connectivity and the ongoing Apple Schools
Initiative."

- ends -

For further information, please contact:
Cathy Pittham/Zoë Smith   or   Frank O'Mahony/Judith Coley
Spreckley Pittham   Apple Computer UK Ltd
Tel: 071-402 3355   Tel: 081-862 3028

Apple and Macintosh are trademarks of Apple Computer, Inc.

Apple Computer

ABOVE   Left, the Acorn memorandum
to staff announcing the launch of ARM,
November 27, 1990. Right, the Apple press
release announcing their investment in ARM,
November 27, 1990.

---

still living there, plus he had kids in a local school and his boat moored on the river, so he
wasn't likely to move any closer to Cambridge.

"It was a gesture on our part to meet Robin halfway, although he did most of the
driving," said John Biggs. "He gave us this bollocking and we couldn't work out whether
he was serious or not, although now I don't think he was; it was a point of principle. The
funny thing is that he's not hard at all, he's as soft as a pussycat in some respects."

John had worked at Acorn during his summer break, but when he graduated
in 1985, the place he had been promised disappeared in one of the company's
regular purges. So he had gone to work for another high technology company, Cray
Computers, which was making supercomputers. But the people in Acorn proved
honorable, and when a place opened up again, he was offered it.

John was the one who had suggested the pub as a meeting place, a decision that
went down well with Saxby, who was used to doing business in pubs — many of the
interviews with potential staff for the fledgling ARM took place in such places. In the
US, deals tend to be done in restaurants such as Il Fornaio, a swish Italian in downtown
San Jose, just across from the Convention Center.

At the time Jamie was essentially the leader of the team. He was the more outgoing
of the senior members of the team and had replaced Steve after he left in August.
Robin had to sort out who these people were, how they fitted together. Jamie, Lee,
Mike and Tudor were running the team between them on an almost aggressively
egalitarian basis, known as the gang of four; the management team was later expanded

RIGHT   The Apple MessagePad, powered by
the ARM610 chip.

and renamed the Gx. What they wanted to do was design the best processors in the
world, not mess about with managing people. They knew that Acorn could no longer
afford its own chip design team, but wanted its own chips designed, and that Apple
desperately needed a replacement for Hobbit that wouldn't cost them a fortune. As
far as the team was concerned, while there was no guarantee that Robin would take
the job — as Tudor explained, "I told Malcolm, 'Yes, he's great but you'll never get him,
he won't want to move to Cambridge'" — they could carry on as they were. Malcolm
had drawn up a business plan that saw the group continue with consultancy, selling the
idea of the processor to people and then customizing it for different applications and
ASIC suppliers. That would allow the team to keep doing what it did best, design chips.
As Tudor says, "Robin's issue was 'What's your vision?' and we didn't have one. We'd
basically spent ten years building brilliant technology that went nowhere and we had
no vision, which was sad."

Eventually, the meeting in the pub went well. Brian O'Donnell quizzed the team
and gave them the thumbs up. Robin asked the team whether they'd agree to spend
money hiring professional management who knew nothing about creating processors,
or whether any of them were willing to be more commercial. Jamie, Tudor, and Mike
raised their hands in the affirmative, and it was agreed that Jamie would run Sales,
Tudor would handle Engineering and Mike would take on Marketing.

His aim, Robin would later claim, was to shake up the team and turn them into the provider of building blocks for the rest of the industry. They would do so through forming partnerships and targeting the embedded market. While companies such as Intel and IBM were the world's dominant providers of processors, Robin recognized that the time for starting such companies had passed. The history of the electronics industry is littered with the skeletons of companies that thought they could do the same thing as Intel or IBM. Instead Robin took ARM down the road of supplying the technology to these companies, large and small, all around the world. It was not just making workstations for high performance computers, but anything else that needed a microprocessor.

That was a huge challenge for a small company in Cambridge with just 12 engineers and one boss, with no salespeople or sales offices anywhere. It required a supreme

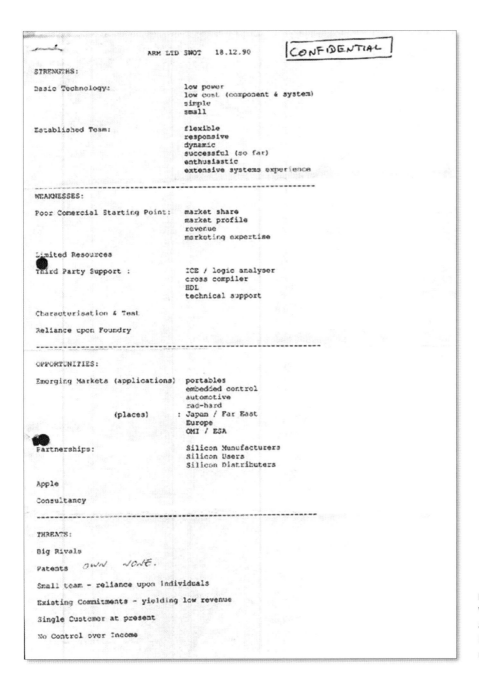

LEFT   The original SWOT (Strengths, Weaknesses, Opportunities and Threats) analysis of the ARM business plan, created December 1990. Note there's no mention of mobile phones.

25×25 John Biggs

YEAR OF BIRTH   1963

COUNTRY OF BIRTH   UK

CITY OF RESIDENCE   Cambridge

UNIVERSITY + DEGREE
Manchester: BSc in Electrical and Electronic Engineering

TENURE AT ARM
1990-

1 Who or what did you want to be when you grew up?   I always wanted to be an Engineer, now I am one.

2 What or who was your first obsession?   My home-built Ohio Scientific Superboard II single-board computer (1979).

3 Who was your childhood hero (or is now)?   My Dad, such a great role model.

4 What's your secret?   If I told you, it wouldn't be a secret!

5 *Star Trek* or *Star Wars*?   Neither, I prefer *The Hitchhiker's Guide to the Galaxy* as it makes me laugh.

6 Did any book change your life? If so, what was it?   *Introduction to VLSI Systems* (1979) by Mead & Conway — it's what got me into chip design at Acorn and hence into ARM.

7 Favorite movie: Monty Python's *Life of Brian* (1979). I have seen it many times and it still makes me laugh out loud.

8 If you could hear only one piece of music again, what would it be?   Echoes (1971), by Pink Floyd

9 Vinyl, cassette, 8-track, CD, MP3, or streaming?   Vinyl.

10 What do you prefer: Skype conference call or face-to-face meeting?   Face to face.

11 Your favorite ARM product is: ARM7TDMI — not only was it a game changer but its royalties paid our salaries for many years.

12 The best use of an ARM product is: Outernet's Lantern — a portable, solar powered, multi-frequency Outernet receiver. It is like 'short wave radio for the digital age'.

13 The best use of an ARM product would be ...   Make the world wide web truly world wide.

14 If you could bring anything back from extinction, what would it be?   Woolly mammoth

15 Your favorite mode of transport is ...   The Lotus twin cam-powered Caterham Super 7 that I built back in 1992

16 What future invention would you like to make (or witness)?   I would like to see a truly sustainable energy source in my lifetime.

17 Ready, Aim, Fire, or Ready, Fire, Aim?   Ready, Aim, Fire — or as I like to put it: 'Measure twice, cut once.'

18 If you could ask one question of anybody, what would it be and to whom?   God: What do you get if you multiply six by nine?

19 When were you happiest?   On my wedding day, surrounded by friends and family.

20 What makes you angry?   Not much — life is too short.

21 What does love feel like?   You know when you know ...

22 Bitcoin or dollars?   Dollars

23 How much is enough?   I once asked my son if he had had enough and he replied that he had had 'lots of nuff'.

24 What is your greatest achievement?   Doing a complete nuts-and-bolts restoration of my father-in-law's 1929 Rolls-Royce.

25 Beach or adventure holiday?   Adventure!

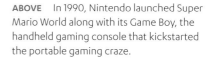

ABOVE In 1990, Nintendo launched Super Mario World along with its Game Boy, the handheld gaming console that kickstarted the portable gaming craze.

belief in their own abilities, a determination to match, and an unusual approach to business — or just wonderful naivety. Of course, the company was created in a different way to most others of their kind. Most often a figurehead puts together a team around a vision, and builds a technology to deliver that vision. Acorn RISC Machines, now renamed Advanced RISC Machines, had a proven technology, a company board of directors and a team, but no figurehead — until Robin passed the audition.

Originally ARM was formed around an off-the-shelf limited company called Widelogic, bought from Companies House for a nominal sum. It appointed directors chosen from the partners: Malcolm Bird for Acorn, Larry Tesler and the head of Apple Europe, Giancarlo Zanni, plus David Mackay, Acorn's legal advisor. The name changed to Advanced RISC Machines Ltd in November 1990, and to ARM Ltd in May 1998.

With the team's approval, and the backing of the board, Robin took the job of managing director in December 1990, although he wouldn't officially join the company until February 1991, as he was still working with ES2. Tim O'Donnell also joined the company, and late in 1990 opened the first US ARM office, in Los Gatos—he and five others, primarily in sales, moved into a building famous for its massive wooden doors, directly adjacent to where Netflix was later founded. In true ARM fashion, the Los Gatos office was within stumbling distance of a sports bar where many a "meeting" was held.

In the interim Jamie fed Robin information about progress, as the group was working on their next-generation processor. Internally it was called the ARM4, until Larry pointed out that Intel had launched the i486 for PCs, and Motorola was working on the 68040 for the Macintosh, and the ARM4 would be following, not leading. So they decided to go straight from the ARM3 to the ARM6, and in doing so announced how far ahead of the game they were.

In December 1990 Robin had the engineers contribute to an analysis of the strengths, weaknesses, opportunities and threats facing the new company. While using a SWOT analysis was unusual back in 1990, including the engineering team in the process was

Acorn
NEWS LETTER

ISSUE 20 LATE SPRING 1991

ARM move to Swaffham

With a level of speed and efficiency that astonished the removal professionals, ARM moved into its new building in Swaffham Bulbeck complete with lock, stock and barrel, just fifteen days after signing the lease.

Most of the preparations for the move were hastily completed in the final days. Up until late January, ARM had been planning to go to Weston Park in Histon. But when the firm in

RAF invests in Acorn

Fighter pilots probably receive some of the most expensive and sophisticated training in the world, second only to astronauts. It's therefore particularly gratifying to learn that 36 Acorn jobs will be playing an important role in the training from now on. The machines have been ordered by RAF Wyton who will also be using the new Acorn indexing system.

Further afield, at Biggin Hill, 96 Archimedes workstations will

Swaffham Bulbeck came suddenly a dilapidated barn. All the old fabric of the 200-year-old building was stripped away until only the timber frame skeleton remained, then reconstructed with concern and steel below being clad with timber and covered with clay peg tiles. The only original part of the building is, as a result, had tenants of furniture and other supplies opening up to see us all through the work. Moving during the push of a recession is no bad thing — we were able to negotiate some very keen deals!

John Marshall supervised the office networking which had to be completed in advance of the move. Special consideration was given to the age of the building and Andy Seale crawled through some very tiny spaces to make

be used to completely to equip the RAF's aircrew selection facility. During a revolts selection process, would-be pilots are subjected to a battery of computer tests and simulations which assess their ability to understand instructions and their overall aptitude for controlling modern fighter planes.

Even further afield ten more Archimedes workstations have been sent to the armed forces in the United Arab Emirates.

note that virtually all the cabling is completely hidden.

Communications during this period was rather chaotic. To begin with there was no phone connected and the there is in a dead area as far as cellular phones are concerned. It gave them no blenger', explains John. 'So that I could call them from Fulborn Road. Then they had to go to the end of the yard with the cellphone to call me and find out what I wanted.

The removal men had remained it would take till midnight to complete the move. By the event, everything was in place by 6 pm, and they sat at the following day to make sure that all the systems were up and running.

'Everyone did their bit', says Robin, 'and I'm especially grateful to David Lowolb who organised everything so smoothly.'

New Zealand to get Acorn Artillery Training Systems

Watching the daily TV coverage of the Gulf War has brought home to many of us the realities of modern warfare. Like the fact that soldiers have to fire their weapons at targets so far in the distance that visual contact is out of the question.

The New Zealand Indirect Fire Trainer (NZIFT) simulates a firing ground complete with realistic scenery, and teaches gunners how to respond to information provided on radar and by observers in the field.

The NZIFT system is based on Archimedes technology and is already used by the British Army. A further five units have now been ordered by the army in New Zealand and Warwick Hunt is very hopeful that further business will be generated in Canada, (which already has one unit in use) and Australia.

ABOVE Breaking the news to Acorn employees that the ARM team was leaving Fulborn Road, and moving to a barn, in Swaffham Bulbeck, a few miles up the road.

---

unheard of. But Robin was very much in favor of transparency, both with staff and with partners, which was very different from Acorn. It wasn't until the team was moving out that an Acorn company meeting was called at the back of the silver building (now ARM2) and staff told what was happening. There was uproar among the employees. They were upset partly because no one apart from the engineers knew what was going on. They also thought the engineering team had forced the split — although John Biggs saw it the other way around, that Acorn was looking to get rid of an expensive team. Some of the people who would remain as Acorn staff were unhappy because they wanted the opportunity to join the startup — especially since all the ARM staff, including the only secretary for the group, Glyn Leonard, were offered share options from the beginning.

The new company needed a new office, and the criteria were quite tough: it had to be within cycling distance of the Acorn premises in Cherry Hinton, a couple of miles outside Cambridge, and it needed to be cheap, so the city center wasn't really an option. Robin was aware that the startup deal was limiting — Acorn had contributed the staff and the designs but no cash. They had £1.5 million from Apple and £250,000 from VLSI Technology, but there was a team of experienced engineers' salaries to pay. Acorn's boss Sam Wauchope had said in public that the deal was saving the company £600,000 a year, so if ARM was ever going to be a sustainable business Robin knew he had precious little time to get the first processor out the door.

Eventually an 18th-century barn in the village of Swaffham Bulbeck, a couple of miles further out of Cambridge, was deemed acceptable to those who cycled. There was nothing in the barn, but it had just been renovated and the owner, David Rayner (owner of Scotsdales, the largest garden center in Cambridge), was anxious to have it rented out, so there was a deal to be made.

Robin set about acquiring furniture from all sorts of places. It's claimed that he won a table for the boardroom on the flip of a coin, but similarly lost a set of desk drawers, leaving one of the engineer's desks without desk storage for several months. This certainly wasn't a swish startup with a swanky office and cash to burn, but a small group of UK engineers looking to compete with well-funded teams of hundreds of designers all around the world.

So on a spring day in March 1991, Lee Smith entered the barn on a Friday with equipment from the office in Acorn, and set it up so that work could start on the Monday.

The team got straight on with redesigning the new chip. The 26-bit address width was a problem for Apple, who wanted a full 32-bit address in order to build more complex systems. So the entire core had to be redesigned. Enter the ARM6: the macrocell, designed for the VLSI Technology process. The ARM60 was the ARM6 processor core with a simple pad ring so it could be packaged as a stand-alone processor. Work was also underway on a hardware floating point unit and an enhanced video chip, VIDC2, which had to be designed for Acorn for use in scientific workstations. However, they took up significant resources in development and testing.

The ARM6xx family were chips that added cache memory and a full virtual memory translation system to the ARM6 core. The ARM610 was the chip that would power both Apple's Newton MessagePad and the next generation of Acorn's Archimedes RISC PC.

But while the engineers were working on the chip design, Robin had other problems. He needed cash, customers and more staff. Moreover he needed a story to sell — and asking the engineers for the SWOT analysis was part of it. These are normally the job of the sales people, but the engineers had the best sense of the company's strengths, and were intellectually honest enough to know its shortcomings.

ARM610

DATE   1992

TECHNOLOGY   CMN12 1.2 μm

TRANSISTORS   358,931

CORE SIZE   7.28 x 7.11 ~= 52 mm^2

FREQUENCY   20 MHz

POWER   120 mW

ARCHITECTURE   ARMv3

uARCHITECTURE   3-stage pipeline with full 32-bit addressing and unified data instruction cache

DESCRIPTION   First full 32-bit address ARM processor and used in the Apple Newton

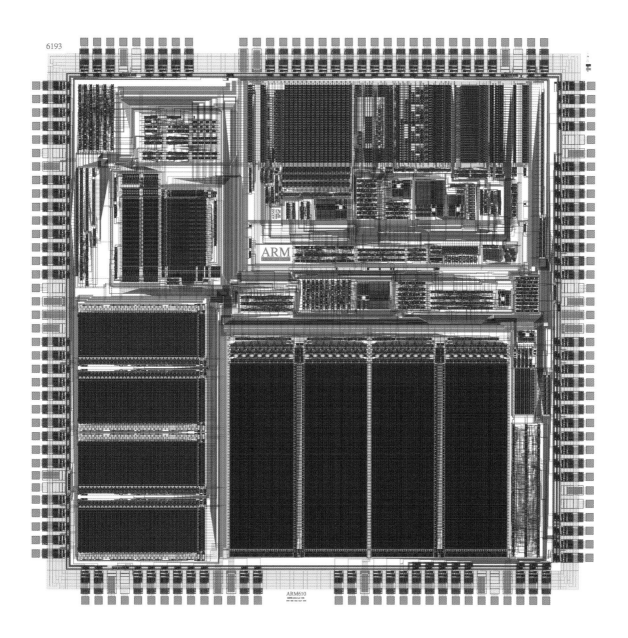

25 × 25 Dave Howard

YEAR OF BIRTH 1959

COUNTRY OF BIRTH UK

CITY OF RESIDENCE Totnes (just outside Cambridge!)

UNIVERSITY + DEGREE University of Reading: Physics & Electronics

TENURE AT ARM 1990-2015

1 Who or what did you want to be when you grew up? A pilot

2 What or who was your first obsession? Dinosaurs (aged ~7)

3 Who was your childhood hero (or is now)? Biggles

4 What's your secret? It wouldn't be secret if I told you

5 *Star Trek* or *Star Wars*? Ham or Cheese? Both!

6 Did any book change your life? If so, what was it? A children's encyclopedia created a thirst for knowledge

7 Favorite movie: *Monty Python's Life of Brian* (1979)

8 If you could hear only one piece of music again, what would it be? So Many Roads by Joe Bonamassa

9 Vinyl, cassette, 8-track, CD, MP3, or streaming? CD

10 What do you prefer: Skype conference call or face-to-face meeting? F-2-F

11 Your favorite ARM product is: ARM7TDMI

12 The best use of an ARM product is: Mobile technology; all that computing/storage/communication that fits in a pocket

13 The best use of an ARM product would be ... Something to fight poverty in the Third World

14 If you could bring anything back from extinction, what would it be? Concorde

15 Your favorite mode of transport is ... Car

16 What future invention would you like to make (or witness)? Viable nuclear fusion to provide clean energy

17 Ready, Aim, Fire, or Ready, Fire, Aim? Ready, Aim, Fire

18 If you could ask one question of anybody, what would it be and to whom? 'Have you even tried it stirred, Mr Bond?'

19 When were you happiest? 1 year ago

20 What makes you angry? Incompetent corporations or government departments

21 What does love feel like? Supportive, reassuring, cozy

22 Bitcoin or dollars? Dollars

23 How much is enough? Enough that you don't need to worry about losing it all

24 What is your greatest achievement? Helping my children grow into respectable adults

25 Beach or adventure holiday? Beach

Robin Saxby, President, ARM Ltd.

‘*ARM designs competitive, high performance, low cost, low power consumption processors; in support of its aims the company develops peripheral cell designs, silicon designs and software tools, and provides design services to third parties.* ’

‘*ARM is targeting the fastest growing sectors of the micro-processor market.* ’

The Company

Advanced RISC Machines Limited (ARM Ltd.) is an independent silicon chip research, design, development and marketing company. It was established in 1990 specifically to service and expand the world market for high performance, low cost, low power consumption, Reduced Instruction Set Computers (RISC).

The Company is new, but the founding partners – Acorn Computers, Apple Computer and VLSI Technology (a licensed manufacturer and design/product partner) – are all well established, successful companies in their own right, with enviable reputations for quality and innovation in their respective fields.

ARM silicon circuits are sold through its semiconductor licensees. ARM Ltd. provides design and consultancy services to the semiconductor licensees and their customers, as well as software and hardware support tools.

The heritage of the ARM product stretches back to 1983, when Acorn started the first commercial RISC chip design. Today ARM chips are available in a range of performance specifications and as a complete family of central processing units (c.p.u.'s),

peripheral devices including memory, video and I/O controllers. ARM circuits are available as off-the-shelf standard components or as macrocells for Application Specific Integrated Circuit (ASIC) design.

Ideal applications are portable products and embedded control.

Today, the original Acorn design team is working for ARM Ltd. This original team has now grown with the addition of equally experienced engineers from other companies, providing a broader experience and application spectrum.

With over 11 versions of ARM chips built, and an installed base of over 145,000 chip sets (580,000 chips), the ARM Ltd. team offers its customers a proven track record second to none.

In order to shorten design cycle time, ARM offers a comprehensive range of development tools including compilers, assemblers and ASIC libraries. ARM provides design consultancy for systems and silicon. Joint and turnkey design is undertaken in both hardware and software.

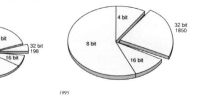

1989   *1995*

Embedded control revenue in $M. 32 bit growth >45% per annum

ARM's major markets are portable products and 32 bit embedded control

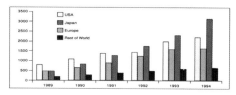

World wide portable shipments in 1000's. Growth >30% p.a.   Source for diagrams, Bader Assocs.

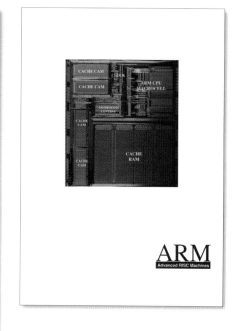

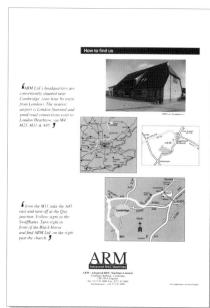

CHAPTER 1 **TO BOLDLY GO …**

49

The ARM design was already highly efficient, mainly as a result of a small team using a simple design. That efficiency delivered a small size — it used around 25,000 transistors, and low power of 120 mW. But ARM had competing requirements from partners. Acorn wanted a powerful, low-cost desktop processor, while Apple wanted a powerful, low power processor. Robin had seen the competition in the desktop market and wanted to head toward embedded designs that were only just emerging.

But at the time everything was about the speed of the processor — how fast you could execute instructions. This was even more important for a RISC system, as you did simple things very fast, so MIPS and IBM were pushing ever-higher speeds. And that was what mattered to Acorn as a desktop system. The lower power simply allowed the cheaper packaging that kept the cost down.

ABOVE The first ARM corporate marketing brochure, given to potential customers, 1991.

ABOVE The first ARM BBQ at the Barn, summer 1991. Clockwise from top left: Dave Jaggar; Alastair Thomas; Pete Harrod and daughter Alison; David Seal (left).

ABOVE   Clockwise from top left: Peng Wong and Glyn Leonard; l-r John Leonard, Tudor Brown, Lee Smith; Serena McLaren and Mike Muller seated in front of one of the ARM SAAB 9000s; Trent Poltronetti holds Robin Saxby's briefcase as Robin sorts out his paperwork.

Another problem identified early on was software. ARM processors only ran the RISC OS operating system developed by Acorn, but not much else. And there weren't that many applications for RISC OS. This suffered in comparison to the range of applications available on Microsoft's Windows, whose latest version, Windows 3.0, launched in August 1990.

ARM still had to identify their target customers. It was one of the key problems for a new company. ARM sold to a chipmaker, who sold to an equipment maker. Robin's job included getting this way of doing business turned around, in order to have an end equipment maker specify an ARM processor core — then several of his customers could bid for the design, and if they wanted to be a part of that design, they had to come to ARM to buy a core. That push-pull approach to the market has always served ARM well.

All of this came together in one theme, the global RISC standard. It became the rallying cry for the company and for customers. It kept Apple and Acorn engaged and flattered their positions as technology leaders, while allowing ARM to go for those other emerging markets where the small size, low cost and low power of their designs would also appeal.

GEC Plessey Semiconductors was an obvious choice as an early customer. Plessey had been in the electronics industry in the UK since the 1960s, and had built some of the first chip fabs in Europe and had provided ULAs, a forerunner to FPGAs used in the design of the original BBC Micro. In 1990 it had been subject to a bruising takeover battle that saw some parts sold off to Siemens, while the semiconductor operation went to GEC, the UK's technology giant through the 1970s and 1980s. It made all manner of electronics, from the first electronic telephone exchanges (through GEC Plessey Telecoms), to washing machines and defense equipment. The problem was the investment required to build the next generation of fabs — the same challenge identified by Morris Chang at Taiwan Semiconductor Manufacturing Company.

Running Plessey, and then GEC Plessey Semiconductors, was Doug Dunn, a straight-talking Yorkshireman. He and Robin got on well. He understood the semiconductor business, bringing that expertise to several other semiconductor firms over the decades. The trouble, though, was that the head of GEC, Lord Weinstock, was notoriously frugal with funds, and the process of actually getting the money would take anything up to six months after the deal was done. If that happened, ARM was dead; time and money were desperately tight.

ARM correctly identified Japanese companies as key potential customers, but perhaps misjudged how long it would take to get them to back this fledgling venture. The team were flying back and forth to Japan almost every month, early in 1991, to meet with companies that could be customers or investors. Japan was the largest supplier of controllers for the embedded market, but these were all 4-bit and 8-bit devices. The highest performance came from 16-bit devices, and they all had their own software development tools and customers who were locked in. Moving to 32 bits was not a priority for them, so ARM struggled.

Another possibility would have been LSI Logic, whose boss, Wilf Corrigan, was British and understood the emerging IP market. But LSI was a direct competitor to VLSI Technology, so off limits. Luckily GEC Plessey Semiconductors, although an ASIC supplier in the UK, wasn't seen as a competitor.

Of course there were also the traditional processor suppliers — National Semiconductor, Motorola and Intel — the relationship with whom would remain a

strain throughout the story of ARM. Intel did everything in-house. Buying in third-party processor designs was not something the engineers at Intel countenanced, especially if it was designed for another chipmaking process, and not fully optimized for its own.

Despite the squeeze on resources, ARM needed more staff, and Robin was clear that they were needed around the world — ARM was not, like Acorn, a very British company, but had to be global from the very start. In early February, while still officially working for ES2 and US2 in California, Robin met with Tim O'Donnell. Or rather, O'Donnell found Robin by the hotel pool and refused to leave until Robin offered him a job. O'Donnell had been at National Semiconductor before joining US2 in 1986 in the design tools group. This had been sold to Cadence Design Systems in 1989 and O'Donnell had gone with the group, as Robin didn't have a role for him in the main company. O'Donnell joined ARM in July 1991, as employee #15. He was paid part time but worked full time from his basement. His task was to talk with potential customers for the core. Although he was the link person for Apple, he was also talking to Texas Instruments and other US chipmakers such as Cirrus Logic. Recruitment continued in Cambridge. ARM employee #16 was a young engineer from Standard Telephones and Cables, named Simon Segars. Robin interviewed him in the pub down the road in Cherry Hinton, which is also where employee #19, a young engineer named Pete Magowan, who had been working at the UK's main processor designer, Inmos, was discovered. He had been in the pub, listening in to Robin talking with Simon. Inmos had been set up with a design center in Bristol in

ABOVE What is claimed to be the inaugural ARM APM, with VLSI the only partner, at the Barn. From the right: Mike Muller (he still owns the cardigan), Jamie Urquhart, Robin Saxby. At the meeting it was decided that single digit numbering be used for a core (ARM6), double digit for a core + JTAG (ARM60), and triple digit for a core + JTAG + cache (ARM600).

25 × 25 Pete Harrod

YEAR OF BIRTH   1955

COUNTRY OF BIRTH   UK

CITY OF RESIDENCE   Cambridge

UNIVERSITY + DEGREE   University of the Witwatersrand: BSc (Eng). UMIST, MSc, PhD

TENURE AT ARM   1990-

1 Who or what did you want to be when you grew up?   Car designer

2 What or who was your first obsession?   Identifying car makes and collecting their registration numbers (I soon grew out of it!)

3 Who was your childhood hero (or is now)?   Nelson Mandela

4 What's your secret?   Not telling

5 *Star Trek* or *Star Wars*?   *Star Wars*

6 Did any book change your life? If so, what was it?   They didn't exactly change my life but *Brave New World* (1932, Aldous Huxley), *Animal Farm* (1944, George Orwell) and *1984* (1948, George Orwell) made a big impression on me as a teenager

7 Favorite movie: *Local Hero* (1983)

8 If you could hear only one piece of music again, what would it be?   Chan Chan (Buena Vista Social Club)

9 Vinyl, cassette, 8-track, CD, MP3, or streaming?   Streaming

10 What do you prefer: Skype conference call or face-to-face meeting?   Face-to-face meeting

11 Your favorite ARM product is: ARM7500FE

12 The best use of an ARM product is: Smartphone

13 The best use of an ARM product would be ...   Self-driving car

14 If you could bring anything back from extinction, what would it be?   Sabre-toothed tiger

15 Your favorite mode of transport is ...   Bicycle

16 What future invention would you like to make (or witness)?   Personal hover-board

17 Ready, Aim, Fire, or Ready, Fire, Aim?   Ready, Aim, Fire

18 If you could ask one question of anybody, what would it be and to whom?   'What's it like?' to the first person to land on Mars

19 When were you happiest?   When my children were born

20 What makes you angry?   Very little

21 What does love feel like?   Wonderful

22 Bitcoin or dollars?   Dollars

23 How much is enough?   3 units a day

24 What is your greatest achievement?   Sticking to 3 units a day

25 Beach or adventure holiday?   Adventure

1978, a fab the other side of the Avon bridge in Newport, Wales, with another in Austin, Texas. It ran the whole process from design to manufacture, including memory chips, and took a very different approach. By 1991 it too had struggled and was now owned by STMicroelectronics. This was a source of good engineers, having taken on a lot of graduates through the 1980s.

The Acorn connection, though, was a tremendous advantage to ARM. Even in New Zealand the BBC Micro was an interesting platform, and inspired a young graduate student there called Dave Jaggar to play with the ARM instructions. His thesis for his master's degree in 1991 was on software that would emulate the ARM instructions on a BBC Micro, so that you could run other software on top, just like you would on the real chip. He was interviewed over the phone and turned up in Cambridge with just £40 in his pocket, ready for his first job and nowhere to live. Mike Muller was in Japan when he arrived, but had arranged for his house keys to be left in the office so that Dave would have somewhere to crash. As employee #18, he developed the ARMulator (ARM emulator) and would also have a major role to play in the future direction of the company.

Meanwhile, after a period spent traveling to Japan and the US every month, Robin recruited a Japanese consultant, Masahiro Konishi, to set up seminars and meetings with the relevant decision-makers. But time and money were running out. ARM needed new customers who would pay a large fee upfront, and new investors who had the same vision.

Before they left Acorn, the engineers had been promised a pay rise in the summer of 1991, and the company was taking on more people. The burn rate was killing them and the staff agreed to hold off on the pay rise. Although Apple and Acorn were happy with the chips they were getting, they were not happy that ARM seemed to be going out of business. It was giving Robin sleepless nights, so he hired a friend, Jonathan Brooks, to find more investors. But as Larry Tesler recalls, Brooks could not find anybody to put a cent into ARM. So at the end of 1991 he said forget it, you won't find anyone.

ABOVE The note left by Mike Muller for Dave Jaggar in 1991, containing details of everything he'd need to know about living in Cambridge. Dave had just arrived from New Zealand.

LEFT The Black Horse, Swaffham Bulbeck 1992. As Mike Muller says, "We were there most days for lunch in the early years — it was only a 200 m walk. We were happy about something, but no one can remember what, perhaps we had just signed the SHARP license." L-r: Robin Saxby, Mike Muller, Pete Harrod, Tudor Brown.

MICROPROCESSOR FORUM

ARM6XX core
3.25 × 2.2 mm
33,494 transistors

ARM
Advanced RISC Machines
VLSI Technology
GEC Plessey Semiconductor

IDT R3081
9.7 × 13 mm
1.3 million transistors

Integrated Device Technology, Inc.

Am29200™
8.56 × 8.76 mm
192,000 transistors

Advanced Micro Devices

National Semiconductor

NS32AM160
7.6 × 7.6 mm
70,000 transistors

HEWLETT PACKARD

PA7100
14 × 14 mm
850,000 transistors

MOTOROLA

88110
14.96 × 14.96 mm
1.3 million transistors

digital™

NVAX
14.6 × 16.2 mm
1.3 million transistors

DECchip 21064
(Alpha AXP)
13.9 × 16.8 mm
1.68 million transistors

TEXAS INSTRUMENTS

SuperSparc
TMS390Z50
15.98 × 15.98 mm
3.1 million transistors

Tsunami
TMS390S10
15 × 15 mm
800,000 transistors

IBM

IBM 486SLC2
7.7 × 9 mm
1.43 million transistors

Cyrix

Cx486DLC/SLC
10.5 × 10.5 mm
600,000 transistors

intel.

Intel386™ SL
13.1 × 13.1 mm
855,000 transistors

Intel960® CF
11.7 × 16.1 mm
818,000 transistors

Intel486™ DX2
6.9 × 11.8 mm
1.2 million transistors

1992

ABOVE At the 1992 Microprocessor Forum there were presentations on 14 chips (each embedded in this lucite obelisk), representing 11 different architectures. By 2015 seven of those architectures were no longer in production, and of the remaining four (ARM, MIPS, SPARC and x86), there's only one clear winner ...

By that time, ARM was within a month or two of running out of money. GEC Plessey signed a license on 31 December, 1991, and if they had not sent the money that day, according to Larry, then the last payroll would have been January 1992. That was very much down to Doug Dunn, who sent the money through anyway, and dealt with the consequences, pointing out that the deal allowed GEC Plessey to make the ARM610 chips for Apple. (He went on to join the ARM board in December 1998.)

All the visits to Japan finally succeeded in securing Nippon Investment and Finance as an investor. Robin was holding this in reserve, though — if the money from GPS didn't come through, then the £650,000 investment from NIF for a 7 percent stake in the company would keep ARM going for another six months. But by the time the NIF money arrived in the middle of 1992, Sharp had also been brought on as a licensee, and the upfront fee had helped to boost ARM's balance sheet.

At the same time, the video games industry was beginning to boom, and companies within the industry started to become possible customers for ARM. The first CD-based games console, 3DO, was taking on Nintendo, Sony and Sega with a business model similar to ARM. Founder Trip Hawkins (he also founded Electronic Arts) had backing from Japanese supplier Matsushita (which also owned the Panasonic brand) for a company that would license the design of the console to manufacturers, and take a royalty from the sale of the design and the software. Matsushita made the chip based around the ARM6 core and a separate floating point unit. Although Sony had initially teamed up with 3DO it pulled out to concentrate on the PlayStation. A second-generation console, the M2, was under development by 3DO using a 64-bit version of the PowerPC chip developed by IBM and Motorola, but the competition from PlayStation killed it off.

When Texas Instruments signed a license in 1993 it proved a turning point for ARM. TI did not have its own general-purpose 32-bit processor but instead focused on digital signal processing (DSP) and 16-bit microcontrollers. It was supplying the DSP chips for Ericsson's mobile phones from its own fabs combined with analog radio components.

Discussions between TI and ARM began in December 1992, after the Microprocessor Forum '92 (in Silicon Valley), where Peter Rheineke of TI saw Mike present the ARM6 family. All conference attendees received an obelisk that contained a chip from all the microprocessors being launched there. Peter was taken by the presentation and thought that the ARM6 core had enough potential for him to approach ARM about licensing it. TI intended using the ARM for automotive applications and for

25 × 25 Lee Douglas Smith

1 Who or what did you want to be when you grew up? Research scientist/theoretical physicist

2 What or who was your first obsession? Understanding how things worked (took a lot of things apart; asked 'Why ... How ... Why ...' obsessively)

3 Who was your childhood hero (or is now)? I never 'did' heroes

4 What's your secret? I don't do secrets

5 *Star Trek* or *Star Wars*? *Star Wars*

6 Did any book change your life? If so, what was it? Lots of books nudged my life a little. You don't want a full list (and I can't remember them all ...)

7 Favorite movie: *Ran* (1985, dir. Akira Kurosawa)

8 If you could hear only one piece of music again, what would it be? Tough question and my answer varies from time to time. Currently Led Zeppelin's Ramble On (1969) or Shostakovich's 5th Symphony

9 Vinyl, cassette, 8-track, CD, MP3, or streaming? CD and vinyl (just bought a new deck!)

10 What do you prefer: Skype conference call or face-to-face meeting? Face to face but everything has a cost. Prefer Skype when cost-to-me (using Skype) < cost-to-me (attending face to face)

11 Your favorite ARM product is: My Surface RT

12 The best use of an ARM product is: Literacy Bridge talking book

13 The best use of an ARM product would be ... I try not to do 'best' — prefer lots of 'good enough'

14 If you could bring anything back from extinction, what would it be? Tyrannosaurus Rex — it would *so* please my son!

15 Your favorite mode of transport is ... Bicycle (or Shanks' pony)

16 What future invention would you like to make (or witness)? I would like to witness useful IoT not funded by advertising, data surveillance, and privacy abuse

17 Ready, Aim, Fire, or Ready, Fire, Aim? Ready, Fire, Aim!

18 If you could ask one question of anybody, what would it be and to whom? 'Er ... who are you?'

19 When were you happiest? As an adult with children (which I still am/have)

20 What makes you angry? People who waste my time for any reason and most especially for no reason

21 What does love feel like? Do you mean 'love' or 'being in love'? They're (very) different. Both answers would be long ...

22 Bitcoin or dollars? Dollars

23 How much is enough? It's enough when your need is met and 'more' has gone asymptotic. When you can no longer taste the difference, stop paying more for the wine!

24 What is your greatest achievement? Far too many not-so-great achievements — very flat landscape for choosing from (what's the highest mountain in Cambridgeshire?). My greatest ARM-related achievement was noticing in December 1990 that we were too unproductive to deliver in July 1991 and doing something about it. Between Tudor (Mr Hardware) and me (Mr Software) we turned it around and delivered ARM6/60/600. Without that joint effort then, we might not exist now.

25 Beach or adventure holiday? Adventure — beaches suck

YEAR OF BIRTH 1952
COUNTRY OF BIRTH UK (England)
CITY OF RESIDENCE Cambridge
UNIVERSITY + DEGREE Cambridge (matric. 1971), MA (Mathematics)
TENURE AT ARM
November 27, 1990-

smartcards. TI has had a long relationship with ARM, with John Scarisbrick, the former head of Europe for TI, joining the board in August 2001. TI was notorious for having a dominant legal department and dictating terms to partners, particularly limiting any announcements about a deal. ARM managed not only to negotiate a successful deal with them, but they included a clause, as with other partners, that allowed them to talk about the deal. That was a huge step for a small company.

Simultaneously ARM signed up Cirrus Logic, a smaller company in the Valley, and launched its ARM7 core. This used the same ARMv3 architecture as the ARM6, but added more support for debugging to make it easier to integrate into a larger chip.

Meanwhile Robin was also talking to a relatively (at this time) unknown Korean company. When Samsung signed up in 1994, no one paid much notice — the deal with AKM (Asahi Kasei Microdevices) in the same year was seen as being more significant — but it was to lead to greater things than even the TI deal.

By 1994 ARM had grown to some 40 people, mostly engineers, with a smattering of support staff, and the barn was bursting at the seams. A row of 18 champagne bottles lined its staircase.

While ARM's prospects were growing, Acorn's were in a terminal decline, and it had lost enough staff by March 1994 that when Acorn moved to smaller premises, ARM could move back to the Water Pumping Station at Cherry Hinton. In some instances employees returned to the same desks they had vacated three years earlier, which might have seemed a small step forward, or even half a step back. But in reality ARM was very much in the ascendency. It wouldn't be long before ARM chips were world-renowned and dominating their industry, helping to power so much invention and revolution in consumer technology around the globe. Less than five years after they'd launched, ARM had struggled and overcome many problems and emerged from its initial phase almost whole. Tragically, though, there had been a huge loss to the team when Al Thomas, the bright star Steve Furber had seen as the next ARM architect, took his own life. His loss hit everyone hard. It was a huge shock, and one that has never been forgotten by everyone at the company — which is why this book is dedicated to him. ▮

ARM7TDMI

DATE	1995
TECHNOLOGY	VLSI "CMN6" 0.6 μm (3-layer metal)
TRANSISTORS	74,000
CORE SIZE	4.0 mm^2
FREQUENCY	33 MHz
POWER	66 mW
ARCHITECTURE	ARMv4T
DESCRIPTION	First 16-bit instruction ARM processor

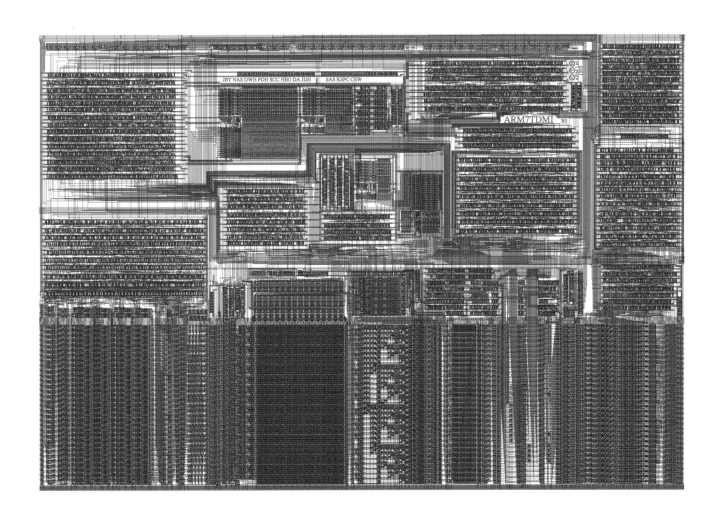

Chip History **1985-2014**

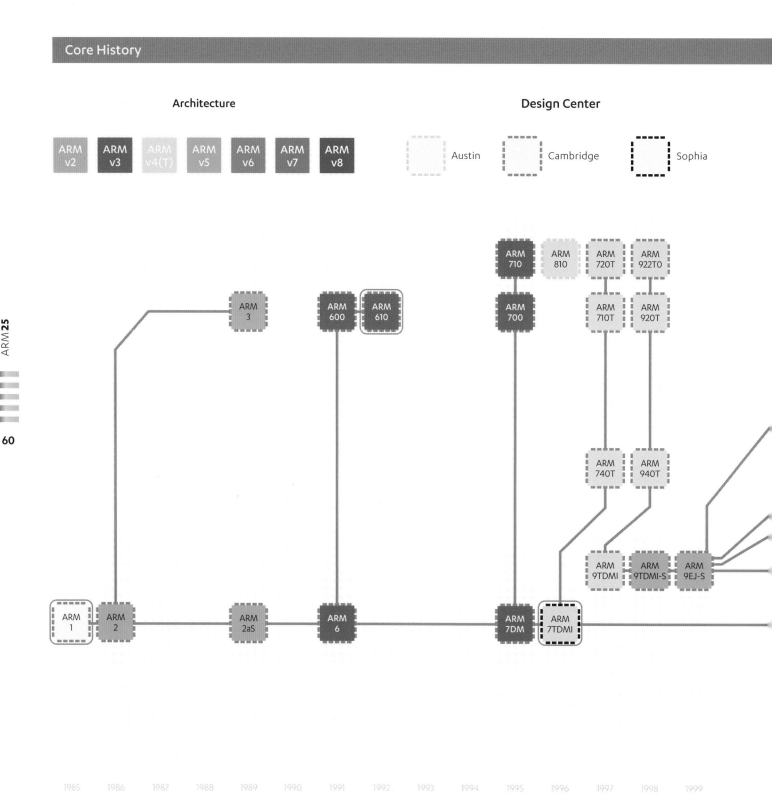

Architecture

ARM v2 · ARM v3 · ARM v4(T) · ARM v5 · ARM v6 · ARM v7 · ARM v8

Design Center

Austin · Cambridge · Sophia

ARM **25**

60

ARM 710 · ARM 810 · ARM 720T · ARM 922T0

ARM 3 · ARM 600 · ARM 610 · ARM 700 · ARM 710T · ARM 920T

ARM 740T · ARM 940T

ARM 9TDMI · ARM 9TDMI-S · ARM 9EJ-S

ARM 1 · ARM 2 · ARM 2aS · ARM 6 · ARM 7DM · ARM 7TDMI

1985 1986 1987 1988 1989 1990 1991 1992 1993 1994 1995 1996 1997 1998 1999

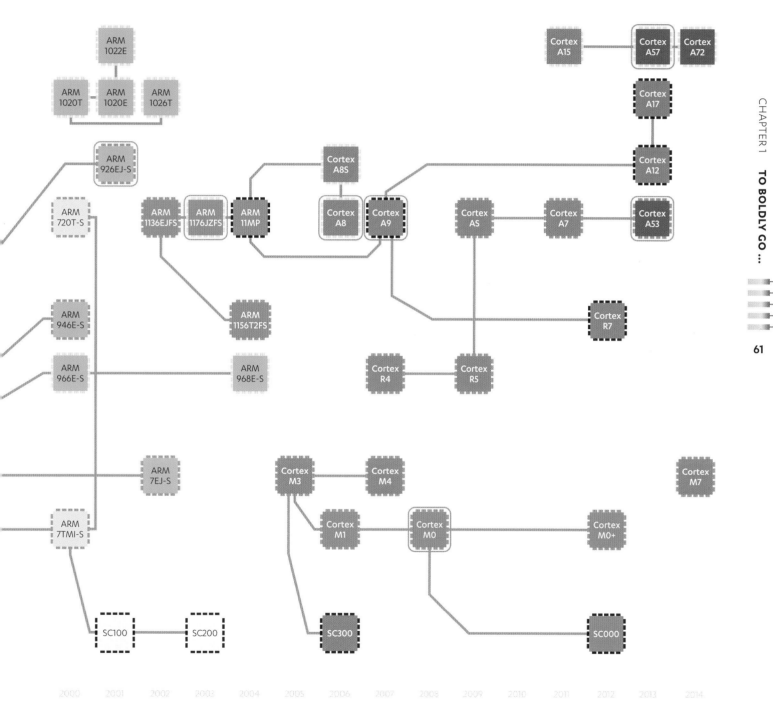

Chapter 2
Don't Panic

Even when you've come so far, what do you do next to invent your own future? By 1994 it was clear that the first showcase products — the Apple Newton MessagePad and the 3DO Multiplayer — had not fared well. The handwriting recognition on the MessagePad was less than impressive, and while the 3DO player had sold 2 million units, that wasn't enough to sustain production. Although Sharp was a partner with Nintendo, the use of an ARM core in the Game Boy had not yet been agreed. However, just after the move back to the original Acorn campus on Fulbourn Road, an unassuming, highly talented engineer called Warren East had been recruited to ARM from Texas Instruments' UK site in Bedford, with a brief to manage the partnership with Sharp on the Nintendo project.

Part of the struggle for 3DO had been its business model, elements of which it shared with ARM. 3DO designed the hardware and licensed it to a range of manufacturers. It also wrote some games, and took a royalty fee from other games companies. Neither, though, was generating enough to invest in the next-generation system (called the M2, and using a PowerPC chip from Motorola rather than an ARM-based chip).

ARM risked being in the same position, without enough licensees to generate sufficient royalties to survive. Like 3DO, ARM was also not in control of which products would succeed and which would not — that was down to the commercial decisions of the partners. Both the Newton and 3DO Multiplayer proved that even great low-power technology wasn't enough to create compelling and successful consumer products.

Even worse, there was a long gap — potentially several years — from the licensing of products to the royalties kicking in. So ARM needed more profile to bring in more licenses to increase the potential for successful, high-volume royalty-generating designs. All of which had to be done without much of a marketing budget. Robin Saxby set out specifically to recruit ARM "evangelists": engineers and executives who could champion ARM technology inside their organizations. He also desperately wanted to match the success of the Intel Inside program, where the component drove what kind of computer you chose to buy. Beginning in 1991, Intel had put millions of dollars behind the program, paying PC makers to include the Intel Inside logo on their boxes. The trouble was, ARM just didn't have that kind of money to spend. Instead, the seeds

LEFT The ARM810 team, posed in front of the silver building.
Back row, l-r: David Seal, David Steer, Stephen Hill, Michael Kilpatrick, Peter Middleton, Kim Rasmussen, Neil Robinson, Nick Salter, Tim Milner.
Front row, l-r: Guy Larri, Chris Wrigley, Ashley Stevens, Ian Devereux, Bill Oldfield, Paresh Jogia, Dave Howard, Harry Oldham.

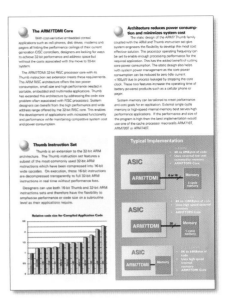

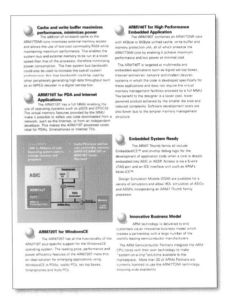

ARM7 Thumb Family
ARM7TDMI, ARM710T, ARM720T and ARM740T

32-bit RISC performance at 8-/16-bit system cost

Product Information

The ARM7 Thumb Family

The ARM7 Thumb family is a range of high performance, low power 32-bit RISC cores incorporating the Thumb 16-bit instruction set extension. This enables 32-bit performance at 8/16-bit system cost.

The family consists of the ARM7TDMI processor core, and the ARM710T, ARM720T and ARM740T cached processor macrocells.

The ARM7 Thumb family is optimized for high-performance but cost-sensitive applications. The range of products has been developed to service different price/performance requirements within the target markets of the portable, embedded and multimedia applications.

The ARM7 Thumb family feature:
- 32-bit register bank
- 32-bit ALU for RISC performance
- 32-bit shifter
- 32-bit addressing (no paging required above 64KB)
- 32x8 DSP multiplier for signal processing
- Thumb instruction set (provides 16-bit code density)

Thumb offers designers
- Excellent code-density for minimal system memory size and cost
- 32-bit performance from 8- or 16-bit memory on an 8- or 16-bit bus for low system cost

ABOVE Original product information for the ARM7 family.

of the "ARM Powered" program were growing, persuading system-on-chip developers, system makers and even consumers that having an ARM processor mattered.

The intention, the need, was to become the global RISC standard. Which wasn't going to be easy. Keeping the two main investors happy while building a sustainable business was also a challenge. Apple and Acorn wanted high performance from ARM, but Robin knew he needed many more licensees in order to make ARM viable long term. On the road frequently, Robin, Mike, Jamie and Tudor visited existing and potential customers across the US, Japan and Asia, while also keeping things running back in Cambridge. This didn't stop Robin's presence being felt in the office, though. His view was that ARM's headquarters was wherever he was with his laptop.

By the middle of 1994 it seemed that ARM faced a fundamental choice: go for premium performance and niche; or embedded, low cost and high volumes.

Fortunately there was a third way that allowed ARM to do both. So far they had licensed the ARMv3 architecture in the form of the ARM6 and ARM7 core

25 × 25 Mike Muller

1 Who or what did you want to be when you grew up? I'll let you know …
Wide Open Road, *Born Sandy Devotional* (1986), The Triffids

2 What or who was your first obsession? Xerox Sigma 9.
Castles Made of Sand, *Axis: Bold as Love* (1967), The Jimi Hendrix Experience

3 Who was your childhood hero (or is now)? The Bromley Crew: H. G. Wells, Peter Kropotkin, Aleister Crowley, Peter Frampton, David Bowie, Topper Headon and Poly Styrene.
Heroes (1978), David Bowie

4 What's your secret? Believe nothing, trust no one.
I'm Not a Man You'd Meet Every Day, *Rum, Sodomy and the Lash* (1985), The Pogues

5 Star Trek or Star Wars? *Star Trek*.
Starbright, *Facing You* (1972), Keith Jarrett

6 Did any book change your life? If so, what was it? *The Illuminatus! Trilogy* (1975), Robert Shea, Robert Anton Wilson.
The Changeling, *LA Woman* (1971), The Doors

7 Favorite movie: *My Life as a Dog* (1985).
Echoes of Primitive Ohio and Chili Dogs, *The Case of the 3-Sided Dream in Audio Color* (1975), Rahsaan Roland Kirk

8 If you could hear only one piece of music again, what would it be? Cry Tuff, *Dub Encounter Chapter 1* (1978), Prince Far I and the Arabs

9 Vinyl, cassette, 8-track, CD, MP3, or streaming? Vinyl. What else gives you music, art and a handy flat surface?
Garvey's Ghost (1976), Burning Spear

10 What do you prefer: Skype conference call or face-to-face meeting? Being alone, but face-to-face if it matters. Wholly Humble Heart, *Gladsome Humour & Blue* (1988), Martin Stephenson and The Daintees

11 Your favorite ARM product is: ARM7TDMI.
Gloria, *Horses* (1975), Patti Smith

12 The best use of an ARM product is: The 1992 Microprocessor Forum Conference give-away on my desk. TI saw my presentation on the ARM6 family and became our third licensee in 1993, which led to the ARM7TDMI design with Nokia for the 8110 and we changed the world.
Lost in the Supermarket, *London Calling* (1979), The Clash

13 The best use of an ARM product would be … Something that changes the world for the better.
Bastard, *Songs for Silverman* (2005) Ben Folds

14 If you could bring anything back from extinction, what would it be? Socialism.
Release the Pressure, *Leftism* (1995), Leftfield

15 Your favorite mode of transport is … A flat bed.
May You Never, *Solid Air* (1973), John Martyn

16 What future invention would you like to make (or witness)? Teleporter.
Future Primitive, *Caravanserai* (1972), Santana

17 Ready, Aim, Fire, or Ready, Fire, Aim? Ready, Fire, Aim.
Screaming Target (1972), Big Youth

18 If you could ask one question of anybody, what would it be and to whom? Deep Thought: 'So explain this 42 thing …'
Marquee Moon (1977), Television

19 When were you happiest? Today.
Higher than the Sun (1991), Primal Scream

20 What makes you angry? Jetlag, people and injustice.
Coffin for Head of State (1981), Fela Kuti and Africa 70

21 What does love feel like? Warm leatherette.
A Love Supreme (1965), John Coltrane

22 Bitcoin or dollars? Bitcoin.
Money (1973), Pink Floyd

23 How much is enough? More than you've got.
You Can't Always Get What You Want, *Let It Bleed* (1969), The Rolling Stones

24 What is your greatest achievement? Helping ARM getting to where it is today.
Boom Shakalaka (1993), Apache Indian

25 Beach or adventure holiday? Beach.
Holiday in the Sun (1977), Sex Pistols

YEAR OF BIRTH	1959
COUNTRY OF BIRTH	UK
CITY OF RESIDENCE	UK
UNIVERSITY + DEGREE	Cambridge University, MA Computer Science
TENURE AT ARM	1990-

implementations for an upfront license fee, with a royalty payable on each chip shipped using the core. Companies such as Samsung paid a higher upfront license fee (which really helped the cash flow in 1994) in return for paying a lower royalty rate later on.

The third way was to also license out the architecture itself for engineers to build their own implementations. This helped the few companies who prided themselves on designing their own microprocessors to overcome their Not Invented Here syndrome. To a certain extent, that didn't make any sense, because the point of ARM's business model was that its customers could employ fewer chip designers, not more. ARM took the effort out of designing a large portion of the chip, allowing them to focus on adding value to their product. However, for these partners, owning the design meant they had more control over their product. As it turned out, the change was to prove a key move, and contributed to ARM earning royalties far into the future.

By 1994, the American computer manufacturer Digital Equipment Corporation was playing catch up with the rest of the industry. It lived in the world of big computers, not the PC. Back in 1977 its founder, Ken Olsen, had notoriously questioned the rationale for the home computer, going as far as to say that "There is no reason anyone would want a computer in their home." However, DEC's VAX and PDP-11 mini-computers had become the mainstay of many corporate operations. It had developed a new, 64-bit RISC architecture, called Alpha, to replace the 32-bit VAX architecture. The first Alpha workstations and servers were launched in 1994; at the Hot Chips conference in Silicon Valley the same year DEC showed the 21164 Alpha chip.

At the same time, ARM was trying to get some good publicity in Microprocessor Report, the industry newsletter (who organized the Microprocessor Forum conference of 1992 that led to ARM's tie-up with TI), that had launched in Silicon Valley in 1987 and which was the bible of high-end processor design and champion of RISC designs. Founder and main writer Michael Slater had reviewed ARM's plans and told them, "I think you've got something pretty good but you need high-end cover, even though it's not your main business." ARM decided that was a good idea, and called a board meeting to talk about who to partner with.

Pretty much at the same time, and out of the blue, DEC called Tim O'Donnell in the US. They said, "We have a lot of excess capacity and we think we need a microprocessor to fill it. We found yours but it's too slow, so our guys were thinking that a design team that did one version of the Alpha are available, we don't want to lose them, so we're thinking that maybe they could do a version of the ARM." DEC had not been a name that the ARM board had mentioned at their meeting to find partners. "We never thought in a million years that they would be interested," as Larry Tesler later recalled.

In the way that engineers do, DEC's team had already started on the design before they called Tim, just to see if it was possible, calling it StrongARM. The engineers were worried about the instruction set and whether it would support things like branch prediction to get higher performance, so the Alpha team decided to do some experiments to make sure it would work. "We were very interested in it, but as cover, not a product, so when Digital wanted a period of exclusivity we said fine," recalled Larry. "The other thing was that we thought we'd learn a lot from them about high speed, and they thought they'd learn a lot from us about low power. But we both admitted it, so we set the deal up so that it was OK to learn from each other. We figured the amounts we would learn would be about equal." The engineers behind that design, led by Dan Dobberpuhl, would play a vital role in the future of ARM devices.

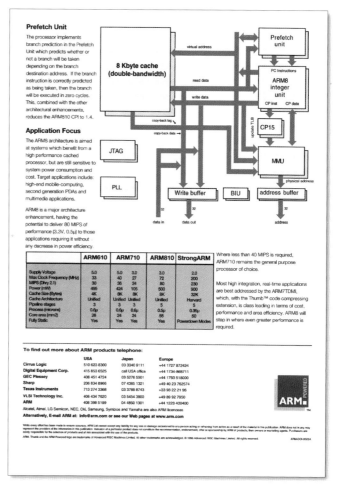

ABOVE The original product brochure for the ARM810.

There was another very important clause in the deal. "We were worried about what would happen if they sold it to one of our licensees, or to one of the Alpha licensees, particularly Samsung," said Larry. "So we had a provision in there that we had to approve the new licensee — and it was lucky we did, as it meant that Intel had to negotiate with ARM to use the part [when Intel acquired DEC some years later]."

It was the start of a steep learning curve for ARM. "There's always a risk when you deal with a company that's 1,000 times bigger than you, but that's true of everything," Larry explained. "That's true of TI, that's true of other licensees; we have some very big companies that are licensees. One thing that I contributed over the years was paranoia over dealing with companies like Intel, Microsoft, and the problems that happened after the deals."

The DEC engineers took the ARM architecture and created an implementation with a five-stage pipeline that could run at up to 200 MHz. The first StrongARM, the SA-110, was launched in February 1996, and used 2.5 million transistors in a die measuring 7.8 mm by 6.4 mm (49.92 mm²). It was built in DEC's 0.36 μm CMOS-6 process at its fab in Hudson, Massachusetts. It met the performance criterion that had been part of the license agreement, intended to ensure that they extended the reach of the ARM architecture to higher performance designs. Later in 1996 they increased its performance to 233 MHz. It would be used in the next generation of Apple's MessagePad, the 2000, as well as in later versions of the Acorn Archimedes and a video

25 × 25 Robin Saxby

YEAR OF BIRTH 1947
COUNTRY OF BIRTH UK
CITY OF RESIDENCE Wooburn Green
UNIVERSITY + DEGREE: Liverpool, B Eng Electronic Engineering 1968
TENURE AT ARM 1991-2007

1 Who or what did you want to be when you grew up?   Own a TV sales and repair shop

2 What or who was your first obsession?   Electrical outfit Christmas present age 8

3 Who was your childhood hero (or is now)?   Mr Birch, a radio ham who died and I inherited his book *The Manual of Modern Radio* (1933) by Scott Taggert, plus his valves and components

4 What's your secret?   It's a secret!!

5 *Star Trek* or *Star Wars*?   *Star Trek*

6 Did any book change your life? If so, what was it?   *The Boy Electrician* (1913), Alfred P. Morgan, and *The Modern Manual of Radio* (1933), Scott Taggert

7 Favorite movie: *Top Gun* (1986) and *The Blues Brothers* (1980)

8 If you could hear only one piece of music again, what would it be?   Boom Boom (1961), John Lee Hooker

9 Vinyl, cassette, 8-track, CD, MP3, or streaming?   Vinyl

10 What do you prefer: Skype conference call or face-to-face meeting?   Face to face with a drink

11 Your favorite ARM product is: iPad (Tesla car on order)

12 The best use of an ARM product is: Helping poor people communicate

13 The best use of an ARM product would be …   Saving mankind from self- or the planet destruction

14 If you could bring anything back from extinction, what would it be?   Tyrannosaurus Rex

15 Your favorite mode of transport is …   Bicycle

16 What future invention would you like to make (or witness)?   Time travel

17 Ready, Aim, Fire, or Ready, Fire, Aim?   Ready Aim Fire

18 If you could ask one question of anybody, what would it be and to whom?   To mankind: How do we improve communication and avoid misunderstanding?

19 When were you happiest?   Every day of my life

20 What makes you angry?   When people lie and make excuses

21 What does love feel like?   Sharing a subliminal understanding with a bit of physicality

22 Bitcoin or dollars?   Swiss francs

23 How much is enough?   Enough to be happy, not too much to be unhappy

24 What is your greatest achievement?   Accidentally skiing off a 50 m cliff doing a 360 degree turn, landing in soft snow on my bottom and only breaking my sunglasses case

25 Beach or adventure holiday?   Adventure

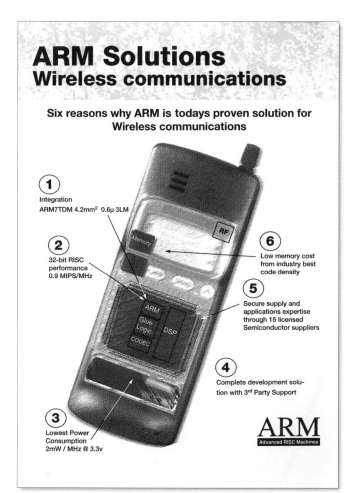

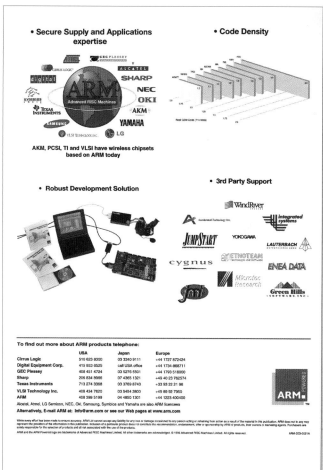

editing system from Eidos. At the same time, ARM was learning a lot from DEC that was useful for its ARM8 development, and the ARMv4 architecture was suited to the longer pipelines to get more performance.

The ARM810 was shown at the Hot Chips conference in Silicon Valley in 1996, as the bridge between the ARM7 and StrongARM. This was the first year an ARM chip had appeared at the conference, where in previous years the show had been dominated by the latest i960 from Intel, the 68060 from Motorola, the PowerPC 604 from IBM and Motorola, or even the ThunderSPARC from Metaflow Technologies. Like StrongARM, the ARM8 used a five-stage pipeline, running up to 55 MHz for the low power performance. However, something was bothering other customers, TI and Nokia in particular. It wasn't performance or clock rate, it was the size of the code that ran on it.

Back in 1994, Tim O'Donnell had approached Larry for technical advice. He was struggling with potential customers who were used to 8-bit and 16-bit code, where the size of the code was a lot smaller. This meant smaller memories and lower system cost. Surely, he thought, since Sophie's original ARM instruction set used a 26-bit program counter to handle the addresses rather than a 32-bit address bus, it couldn't be too hard. Larry suggested putting a general-purpose emulator into the ARM chip to emulate 8- or 16-bit code, so Tim ran that by Mike Muller, who called it "a terrible idea." Larry said, "come up with a better one," and every time O'Donnell raised it with the engineers they'd say, "We think we can convince them to rewrite the code in ARM instructions."

ABOVE Marketing material from the late 1990s, using a mocked-up, non-brand-specific phone image. ARM begins to take a segment view of the market.

Nokia were looking for a new line of digital mobile phones with a more sophisticated display, and it needed a high performance, low power general-purpose processor that could be integrated with other components such as the DSP. A British project manager at Nokia had picked up the latest issue of Acorn User magazine at an airport in which a feature had highlighted the ARM core used in the Archimedes PC. So they looked at the ARM7DI, but the 32-bit code, while more compact than other 32-bit architectures, wasn't as good as the existing 16-bit implementation they were using from Hitachi.

Following a depressing trip back from Finland after failing to convince Nokia to move to the ARM7DI, Dave Jaggar, the New Zealand engineer with an intimate knowledge of the instructions as part of the ARMulator development, sketched out a way to encode a set of 32-bit instructions using only 16 bits. The key was that it used an extra block of transistors at the start of the process, so that code didn't need to be rewritten. In a nod to the increasing use of ARM as a word rather than an acronym, this became known as Thumb. The team returned to Finland, and convinced Nokia and TI to take a gamble that ARM could add Thumb to the ARM7TD and deliver ARM7TDMI on an aggressive schedule, in order to meet their projected new product launch.

Thumb turned out to be vital to the success of the development of the next generation of digital mobile phone chips. In March 1995, it was announced to the world, targeting "mobile phones, pagers and disk controllers [that] require more performance, address space and software support than 8- or 16-bit controllers can deliver." ARM's PR blurb attacked its own products, saying "while 32-bit systems are fast enough, they may be too expensive for consumer markets, since they require more memory and a more complex circuit board."

Thumb reduced the typical program size by 30-40 percent from ARM's already good code density, which was great for designers where memory was tight.

The press release that announced the launch of Thumb took pains to point out this wasn't an emulation approach. "All Thumb aware processor cores combine the capability to execute both the 32-bit ARM and the 16-bit Thumb instruction sets. Careful design of the Thumb instructions allows them to be decompressed into full ARM instructions transparently during normal instruction decoding without any performance penalty. This differs from other 32-bit processors implementing a 16-bit data bus, which require two 16-bit memory accesses to execute every 32-bit instruction ("SX" style) and so halve performance." The industry response was positive. Jim Turley, senior editor on the Microprocessor Report, wrote that, "For price-sensitive embedded applications, Thumb is a clever and unique solution. It keeps all the advantages of ARM's low-power 32-bit RISC architecture and adds the benefits of code density that 16-bit designers expect."

The ARM7TDMI was based on a new variant of the ARMv4 architecture, ARMv4T, incorporating Thumb. It used just 75,000 transistors and, in a similar 0.35-µm process to the StrongARM, measured just 2.1 mm^2. It included more multipliers for digital signal processing ("M") as well as the debug ("D") and the in-circuit emulator ("I") than the previous version.

"The development of Thumb reaffirms ARM's leadership as the global volume RISC standard," said Robin at the time, pushing the branding he hoped would keep Apple and Acorn happy. As this came just a month after the announcement of the StrongARM partnership with DEC, which would end up in both their designs, this was giving him both the high-end cover and the low-end market.

The industry's knowledge of Nokia's adoption of Thumb for future products helped to make it a success, and attracted new licensees to ARM, including Mietec, the chip design subsidiary of French telecoms giant Alcatel. This was a big deal for ARM: a major industry player validating their technology against all the other contenders.

Vincent Roland, marketing director at Mietec, said at the time, "We made a study of all possible embedded processors on the market, including MIPS, SPARC, Intel and Motorola, and found the ARM to be 20 to 30 percent better in benchmark tests." It was the beginning of greater things, and Larry's paranoia about large US companies was soon put to the test, when ARM managed to land a customer that was expected to be extremely significant: Microsoft. As the largest operating system supplier on the planet, it was a major player in the industry.

Windows CE was announced at the Comdex (Computer Dealers Exhibition) show in 1996 as the operating system for the portable system. It had released a reference platform to several hardware partners during 1995, using the SH3 from Hitachi or the MIPS 3000 or MIPS 4000 core from MIPS licensees. ARM seemed a glaring omission from their list, but partners VLSI and Cirrus Logic weren't engaged with Microsoft. Robin swung into action, meeting with Microsoft to see how Windows CE could be ported to the ARM architecture. The trouble for ARM, though, was that Microsoft's other architectures were backed by companies with deeper pockets, and they could pay for operating system development. It was something of a bigger problem for ARM, since no single licensee was likely to pay for development that would benefit all of its competitors. ARM couldn't afford to pay for it if it only benefited a couple of licensees.

ABOVE   Original product information for the ARM9 family. Java had become an important development language for cellphones.

The result was stalemate — until 1997, that is, when Microsoft announced that Windows CE2.0 included support for ARM, especially the StrongARM. The intention was to open up a wide range of designs for portable computers using the PocketPC format. It would bring ARM and its chipmaking partners to a wider set of system manufacturers, such as Compaq, HP, LG and many others.

The previous year had seen the launch of another portable form factor: the Palm Pilot. Developed by Palm and acquired by US Robotics in 1995, the original Palm Pilot was seen as the first usable personal digital assistant, running off two AAA batteries for months, and powered by Motorola's DragonBall 68000 processor. A color version in 2002, called the Tungsten, would adopt the ARM architecture, and the Palm Treo in 2002 was one of the first true smartphones, powered by a 144 MHz ARM OMAP1 processor from Texas Instruments.

The ARM7TDMI had been created to satisfy the requirement of Nokia; eventually in late 1996 the first ARM-powered Nokia phone, the 8110, was launched. Often referred to as the Banana phone due to its unique curved design, the cover slid open to reveal the keyboard. Unfortunately, though, if you kept one in a pocket or purse the slider would fill with dust and become difficult to open.

The Nokia's 6110 release, in December 1997, introduced the world to Snake; this phone, with its robust design, long battery life and a wide range of accessories was a key step along the road to Nokia's domination of the cellphone business. Powered by the ARM7TDMI core in the Nokia-designed ASIC MAD (Microcontroller And DSP) it would also propel ARM to great success.

From a UK perspective, though, in the mid-1990s there was another player in the portable computer market. Psion, founded in 1980 by South African entrepreneur David Potter, had been a leader in portable computers since its Organiser launched in 1984. They launched their Psion Series 3 handheld computer, which was based around an SH2 processor from Hitachi in 1993. For the 1997 launch of the Series 5 (like ARM, there was no Series 4), Psion introduced an innovative sliding keyboard (which helped it become immensely popular) and a full 32-bit design with a new processor, the ARM7 from Cirrus Logic. A new processor architecture meant a new operating system, and EPOC32 was developed with a full file system and support for modems. All of this came in a pocket-sized device that could run for a couple of weeks before the two

BELOW The Nokia 6110, with which ARM and Nokia changed the world.

RIGHT The Nokia 8110 (1996), powered by the ARM7TDMI chip, was known as the Banana phone due to its curved shape. It starred in *The Matrix* (1999).

25 × 25 Simon Segars

1 Who or what did you want to be when you grew up?   A photographer

2 What or who was your first obsession?   Trying to build things

3 Who was your childhood hero (or is now)?   Sorry, I've never really done hero worship

4 What's your secret?   Like I'm going to tell you!!

5 *Star Trek* or *Star Wars*?   *Star Wars*

6 Did any book change your life? If so, what was it?   A science dictionary I bought when I was about 10

7 Favorite movie: *Star Wars IV* (the original and best!)

8 If you could hear only one piece of music again, what would it be?   Something classical and peaceful

9 Vinyl, cassette, 8-track, CD, MP3, or streaming?   Streaming

10 What do you prefer: Skype conference call or face-to-face meeting?   f2f

11 Your favorite ARM product is: My Tesla

12 The best use of an ARM product is: Connecting the planet

13 The best use of an ARM product would be …   Enabling 8 billion people to coexist without ruining the planet or each other

14 If you could bring anything back from extinction, what would it be? Velociraptor, just for fun

15 Your favorite mode of transport is …   London underground

16 What future invention would you like to make (or witness)?   Teleportation

17 Ready, Aim, Fire, or Ready, Fire, Aim?   Ready, Aim, Fire

18 If you could ask one question of anybody, what would it be and to whom?   Albert Einstein, what makes you tick?

19 When were you happiest?   When the gamble pays off

20 What makes you angry?   When technology gets in the way

21 What does love feel like?   Safe. And dangerous

22 Bitcoin or dollars?   Bitcoin

23 How much is enough?   I'll let you know

24 What is your greatest achievement?   My family

25 Beach or adventure holiday? Beach

YEAR OF BIRTH   1967
COUNTRY OF BIRTH   England
CITY OF RESIDENCE   Palo Alto
UNIVERSITY + DEGREE   Sussex (BEng Electronic Engineering), Manchester (MSc Computer Science)
TENURE AT ARM   1991-

AA batteries needed replacing. A year later, Psion and phone manufacturers Ericsson, Motorola and Nokia spun out Symbian as a new joint venture company, with EPOC32 as the operating system for their smartphones.

The seeds for this ARM success had been planted back in 1995, when they knew that they had to add a lot more around the processor core to make things work. Gone were the days of the VIDC, MEMC and IOC chips that sat alongside the core. For the embedded market there now needed to be a bus interconnect to a wide range of peripherals. Through that year, the engineers at ARM were developing a key piece of technology that allowed the processor core and memory to work more efficiently, both together and with other peripherals on the chip. The advanced microprocessor bus architecture (AMBA) would turn out to be so effective that other companies would license it to use with other processors — for example Infineon later used the AMBA technology with a MIPS processor core.

The first two pieces of the technology were the Advanced System Bus, connecting up the core and memories, and the Advanced Peripheral Bus, to link to the rest of the system. AMBA, with its second and third generations in 2001 and 2003, would form a key extension of ARM's business into other parts of the chip.

At the same time, the financial future of the company was of some concern. The company had weathered a rocky start with the help of a friend of Robin's, named Jonathan Brooks. Back then Jonathan had pointed out that the company couldn't afford to employ Robin, let alone him, but by 1995, with Samsung, TI and DEC onboard as additional licensees, ARM had earned some breathing space. Jonathan was taken on as finance director, and plans were made for some financial engineering.

His appointment coincided with the company making its first major investment, into Palmchip. ARM took a 45 percent stake in the company in 1997, less than a year after its startup by a former Samsung engineer in the US. It was developing CoreFrame, a series of components designed to sit around the processor in a system-on-chip, and was targeting both ARM and MIPS. ARM's stake was sold a few years later for a $500,000 profit.

But the big financial opportunity envisioned for ARM was a public listing. Launching as a public company on a stock exchange offered anyone with enough money the chance to buy ARM shares that were held at the time only by the founders and initial investors. It would also allow staff to use their options to buy shares and sell them, hopefully, at a profit. It was, of course, a big undertaking. There were several merchant banks that could help with an initial public offering, and there were other banks that would potentially buy the shares once the company went public. But ARM was not like other startups, which tended to have venture capital funds as investors pushing for an IPO. ARM's backers were the large corporations Apple and Acorn.

Meanwhile, back in Cambridge, sales of the ARM8 family had stalled (processor pun intended). Although it incorporated some of the learning from the StrongARM group, it was neither high enough performance, nor low enough power. Simultaneously and separately, Steve Furber at the University of Manchester was experimenting with even lower power implementations of the ARM architecture. Amulet2e was an asynchronous design where there was no central clock making sure all the blocks ran at the same time. Instead, calculations rippled through the chip at their own speed, to be brought together at the end. This approach could potentially reduce the power consumption even further, with Steve showing that it could provide performance of 40 MIPS with just 150 mW.

This was the first full asynchronous processor with cache and memory controller, and was first presented by Jim Garside at the Hot Chips conference in August 1996. It bore comparisons to the ARM7 and ARM8 chips, with silicon developed by VLSI providing nearly twice the performance of the ARM7, and a better MIPS/Watt figure than the ARM810. However, the increased complexity of system design and problems with manufacture meant that asynchronous designs have never become part of the mainstream.

Throughout 1996, the CPU team led by Simon Segars were focused on developing the next family, ARM9. It was duly launched in 1997 at the Microprocessor Forum, with the ARM9TDMI integer processor core and the ARM940T, a full processor with 4 KB instruction and data caches. Four of the existing partners took up licenses in 1997, marking a significant boost after the ARM810.

The team had also been working on a new version of the wildly popular ARM7. Until then it had essentially been a "black box" dropped into a customer design — where the design had to be ported to each new manufacturing process. The disaggregation of the semiconductor manufacture chain was well underway, driven by the rise of the foundry model. But most semiconductor companies still owned their own fabs, each using their own unique process. By the middle of 1997, there were 35 different ports of the ARM7TDMI, on processes ranging from 0.72 μm to 0.35 μm, all of them needing lots of engineering support. The launch of a synthesizable version changed everything. It tapped into the newer design approach of synthesis, where all the elements of a chip design could be described at a high level using what was essentially a programming language. This moved the challenge of chip development away from designing at the transistor level, and raised it to creating blocks of code using Verilog or VHDL (both high level description languages). The ARM7TDMI core was rewritten in Verilog and initially used by LSI Logic for customers such as storage systems maker Emulex. Also in 1997, Rockwell licensed the ARM7 technology in a move that would have major repercussions, as modems moved from fixed designs to programmable, allowing faster speeds. All this was part of the growing impact of the Internet. Although only available via dialup to the home, there was increasing focus on the telecoms and networking infrastructure, using high performance cores such as SPARC and MIPS where power was not such an issue.

Later in the year came another huge shift in the market for ARM. In May 1997, DEC sued Intel, claiming Intel's x86 microprocessors the Pentium, Pentium Pro and Pentium II processors had infringed 10 DEC patents. By the end of the year, though, DEC had sold its semiconductor business to Intel for $700 million, including the StrongARM line and the fab where it was made (to replace the aging i860 and i960 RISC processors). Under the terms of the architectural license, Intel now had to come to ARM to continue to use the StrongARM products. This was very much a case of Goliath having to come to David. And, since a publicity clause in the original contract with DEC allowed it, ARM could tell the world that Intel was a licensee. Which it did.

Subsequently the Xscale architecture was born, combining with Windows CE in the PocketPC format from manufacturers such as Asus, HP and even Intel's own Web Tablet design (which never saw the light of day).

It's an indication of the company's ambition that despite shipping 10 million processors from eight partners and signing six new ARM7TDMI licensees (including Matsushita, Seiko, Epson, Toshiba and HP), ARM regarded 1997 as a difficult year.

But, with lots of positive numbers, and more partners waiting to sign up, the decision was made by the board to go for an IPO in 1998 and go on a global "roadshow,"

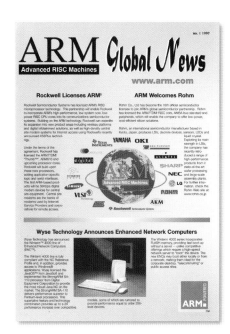

ABOVE   The debut issue of the ARM official publication, 1997.

CHAPTER 2   **DON'T PANIC**

77

25 × 25 Warren East

YEAR OF BIRTH 1961
COUNTRY OF BIRTH UK
CITY OF RESIDENCE Cambridge
UNIVERSITY + DEGREE Oxford, Engineering Science
TENURE AT ARM 1994-2013

1 Who or what did you want to be when you grew up? A solicitor for a while, then a captain of industry

2 What or who was your first obsession? Trains

3 Who was your childhood hero (or is now)? Characters from *Swallows and Amazons* (1930), Arthur Ransome

4 What's your secret? I'm not really mean, it's just an act

5 *Star Trek* or *Star Wars*? *Star Wars*

6 Did any book change your life? If so, what was it? No, I'm nearly illiterate

7 Favorite movie: *The Lord of the Rings* series (2001-2003)

8 If you could hear only one piece of music again, what would it be? *Toccata* from Widor's 5th Symphony

9 Vinyl, cassette, 8-track, CD, MP3, or streaming? MP3 now, lots of wasted vinyl

10 What do you prefer: Skype conference call or face-to-face meeting? Face-to-face

11 Your favorite ARM product is: iPhone

12 The best use of an ARM product is: Photonstar lights

13 The best use of an ARM product would be ... Implanted vital signs sensor

14 If you could bring anything back from extinction, what would it be? Mega tree from carboniferous period

15 Your favorite mode of transport is ... Boat

16 What future invention would you like to make (or witness)? Low cost holographics

17 Ready, Aim, Fire, or Ready, Fire, Aim? Ready, Aim, Fire

18 If you could ask one question of anybody, what would it be and to whom? Einstein: 'talk me through the thought process'.

19 When were you happiest? With a young family

20 What makes you angry? When I procrastinate

21 What does love feel like? Great

22 Bitcoin or dollars? Bitcoin

23 How much is enough? Never enough

24 What is your greatest achievement? Helping ARM

25 Beach or adventure holiday? Adventure

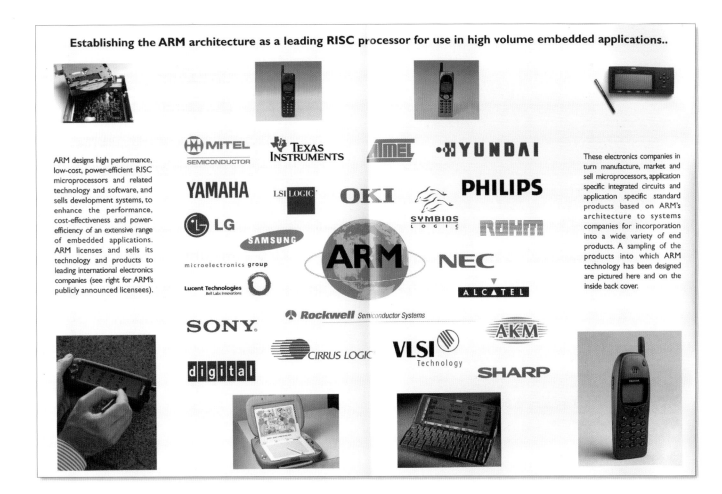

Establishing the ARM architecture as a leading RISC processor for use in high volume embedded applications..

ARM designs high performance, low-cost, power-efficient RISC microprocessors and related technology and software, and sells development systems, to enhance the performance, cost-effectiveness and power-efficiency of an extensive range of embedded applications. ARM licenses and sells its technology and products to leading international electronics companies (see right for ARM's publicly announced licensees).

These electronics companies in turn manufacture, market and sell microprocessors, application specific integrated circuits and application specific standard products based on ARM's architecture to systems companies for incorporation into a wide variety of end products. A sampling of the products into which ARM technology has been designed are pictured here and on the inside back cover.

presenting the company to various financial organizations in London, New York and Tokyo. Consumer companies with global intentions follow an IPO process in which they generate a lot of hype for the public to stimulate sales — but that was not a route that ARM considered, because they intended to sell shares to institutional investors, not members of the public. So meetings were set up with the technical press, all of whom were well aware of ARM. The national and general business press was less interested, and generally didn't understand what ARM did.

After conducting what is commonly called a "beauty parade" of merchant banks for the job of conducting their flotation, the ARM board selected US bank Morgan Stanley Dean Witter, which dominated the technology landscape at the time. Being a UK company with a global business proved something of a challenge for the financial markets. American investors — including Apple — wanted the shares to be available on the Nasdaq stock exchange, or, failing that, the New York Stock Exchange. Which was where companies such as Intel, AMD, Dell, HP, Cisco and WorldCom were hosted. But Nasdaq did not admit foreign companies at the time of the ARM float, and there was no appetite to move ARM to America. (Nasdaq allowed listings of non-US-based companies from January 1998, but only under stricter criteria than US companies.) So the London Stock Exchange was the natural choice. Robin wanted to make sure that the focus was global, though, so the company restructured as ARM Holdings. This allowed a dual listing, issuing shares in London as well as using American Depository Shares on Nasdaq. This type of US listing allowed for US dollar-denominated equity shares (each of

ABOVE   In the lead-up to the ARM stock market flotation the company advertised its partners and the tech innovations it had created.

which represented three shares held back in London) to be available for purchase on an American stock exchange.

The road to the IPO wasn't without its troubles, though. Acorn temporarily halted it, because they wanted the ARM management to undertake a reverse takeover of Acorn, which was already a UK listed company with a share price primarily based on its share holding in ARM. This reverse takeover would have been tax efficient for the Acorn shareholders, but would have left the ARM management with the challenge of disposing of the failing Acorn business. In an aggressive move — which left some of the founders with deep reservations about future joint ventures — the ARM management were all served with legal notices reminding them of their fiduciary duty to their shareholders in considering any course of action, and the possible ramifications should they not do this. The team duly considered the best course of action for all the shareholders, and, with the support of Apple and VLSI Technology, put the IPO back on track.

The dual listing almost killed the IPO, too. When Robin arrived in New York for the launch on Nasdaq he was told that ARM's employee share options were legal for London but they contravened the Nasdaq regulations. So more money had to be put aside to allow for them, but once that was confirmed, the flotation was back on.

On April 17, 1998, ARM Holdings floated 11 million shares on the London Stock Exchange and Nasdaq at £5.75 each in London and $29 in the US. The IPO valued ARM at £264 million, raising £33 million for existing shareholders Acorn, Apple and VLSI, plus the founders. The shares rocketed in value, even though the launch price of $29 was already well ahead of market expectations of $19. The price rose to over $42 that day, giving a huge vote of confidence in the technology, the intellectual property (IP) model, and the foundry business.

RIGHT   The world's first wrist watch with built-in GPS was launched by Casio in January 1999.

LEFT   Larry Page and Sergey Brin, founders of Google, in 1998. The company proved to have a viable web-based business model that survived the rapidly approaching dot.com crash, and later disrupted the mobile phone industry with the introduction of Android.

The very same day saw another tech star float on Nasdaq. Broadcom had been started in 1991, by Henry Samueli and Henry Nicholas, in an apartment in southern California (not Silicon Valley). They had also seen the opportunity offered by the foundry model, and were designing demodulator chips for TV set-top boxes. They then turned to Fast Ethernet chips and were a key part of the growth of connecting devices for Internet access. Theirs was a more traditional chip startup, with backing from venture capital as well as investment by customers such as Intel, Cisco and General Instrument. Merchant bank Morgan Stanley Dean Witter underwrote the flotation, as it did with ARM. Broadcom floated at $24, with shares changing hands for over $60 later in the day, and was called the hottest deal of the year.

The two flotations were a part of the Internet bubble, a period later defined as "irrational exuberance" by Alan Greenspan, the chairman of the US Federal Reserve. Typically massive valuations of Internet stocks such as boohoo.com, broadcast.com and Geocities.com overshadowed the growth of companies building the information infrastructure, such as Cisco and WorldCom.

Back in Cambridge, for the first time there was a lot of money available to ARM founders. One of them bought a new house and didn't realize, until after the deal was

PROSPECTUS (Subject to Completion)
Issued March 17, 1998

11,730,000 Shares

ARM Holdings plc

IN THE FORM OF ORDINARY SHARES OR AMERICAN DEPOSITARY SHARES

Of the 11,730,000 ordinary shares, nominal value 1p per share (each a "Share"), of ARM Holdings plc (together, where the context so requires, with its subsidiaries, the "Company" or "ARM") being offered, 5,865,000 Shares are being offered initially in the United States and Canada by the U.S. Underwriters (the "U.S. Offering") and 5,865,000 Shares are being offered initially outside the United States and Canada by the International Underwriters (the "International Offering" and, together with the U.S. Offering, the "Offering"). See "Underwriters". Of the 11,730,000 Shares being offered, 5,885,000 Shares are being issued by the Company and 5,845,000 are being sold by the Selling Shareholders named herein. See "Principal and Selling Shareholders". The Company will not receive any of the proceeds from the sale of Shares by the Selling Shareholders. The Shares offered hereby may be sold in the form of ordinary shares, or upon request in the form of American Depositary Shares ("ADSs"), each ADS representing three Shares. The ADSs will be evidenced by American Depositary Receipts ("ADRs"). Prior to the Offering, there has been no public market for the Shares or ADSs. It is currently anticipated that the initial public offering price will be between 325p and 385p per Share, equivalent to between $16.24 and $19.24 per ADS, translated at £1.00 = $1.6658 (the Noon Buying Rate (as defined herein) on March 13, 1998). For a description of the factors to be considered in determining the initial public offering price, see "Underwriters".

The ADSs have been approved for quotation, subject to official notice of issuance, on the Nasdaq National Market under the symbol "ARMHY" and application has been made for the Shares to be admitted to the Official List of the London Stock Exchange.

SEE "RISK FACTORS" BEGINNING ON PAGE 7 HEREOF FOR A DISCUSSION OF CERTAIN FACTORS THAT SHOULD BE CONSIDERED BY PROSPECTIVE INVESTORS.

THESE SECURITIES HAVE NOT BEEN APPROVED OR DISAPPROVED BY THE SECURITIES AND EXCHANGE COMMISSION OR ANY STATE SECURITIES COMMISSION NOR HAS THE SECURITIES AND EXCHANGE COMMISSION OR ANY STATE SECURITIES COMMISSION PASSED UPON THE ACCURACY OR ADEQUACY OF THIS PROSPECTUS. ANY REPRESENTATION TO THE CONTRARY IS A CRIMINAL OFFENSE.

| | PRICE $ | AN AMERICAN DEPOSITARY SHARE AND | P A SHARE | |

	Price to Public	Underwriting Discounts and Commissions (1)	Proceeds to Company (2)	Proceeds to Selling Shareholders (2)
Per ADS	$	$	$	$
Per Share	p	p	p	p
Total (3) (4)	$	$	$	$

(1) The Company and the Selling Shareholders have agreed to indemnify the Underwriters against certain liabilities, including liabilities under the Securities Act of 1933, as amended. See "Underwriters".
(2) Before deducting estimated expenses of approximately $2,890,000 payable by the Company and $ payable by the Selling Shareholders, respectively.
(3) Translated at the rate of £1.00 = $ (the Noon Buying Rate (as defined herein) on   , 1998).
(4) The Company and the Selling Shareholders have granted to the Underwriters an option, exercisable within 30 days of the date hereof, to subscribe for and/or purchase up to an aggregate of 1,759,500 additional Shares at the price to public less underwriting discounts and commissions, for the purpose of covering overallotments, if any. If the Underwriters exercise such option in full, the total price to public, underwriting discounts and commissions, proceeds to the Selling Shareholders and proceeds to the Company will be $, $, $ and $, respectively. See "Principal and Selling Shareholders" and "Underwriters".

Global Coordinator
MORGAN STANLEY DEAN WITTER

The ADSs and the Shares are offered, subject to prior sale, when, as and if accepted by the Underwriters named herein and subject to approval of certain legal matters by Shearman & Sterling, counsel for the Underwriters. It is expected that delivery of the ADRs evidencing the ADSs and of the Shares will be made on or about   , 1998, (i) in the case of the ADRs through the facilities of the Depository Trust Company and (ii) in the case of the Shares through the facilities of CRESTCo Limited, in each case against payment therefor in immediately available funds.

MORGAN STANLEY DEAN WITTER
      COWEN & COMPANY
                  HAMBRECHT & QUIST

, 1998

done, it was the most expensive in Cambridge at the time. Another bought a new vacuum cleaner. The money wasn't that important to many of them, although soon enough a Porsche or two started appearing in the car park at Fulbourn Road

Naturally, some people had missed out on the success of the IPO. The company had grown from employing 30 people to over 350 in just four years, but a few had left, giving up their share options when they did so. When some of them returned later they had to face being teased by Robin about the cash and options they missed out on. But there were also those who had been at the company from the beginning, and who had always believed in what they were capable of. They quietly and calmly got on with the business of doing what they loved most.

While the IPO marked a turning point for the future of ARM, essentially giving it more funds for growth, the business of processor design continued as relentlessly as it always had.

25 × 25 Allen Wu

1 Who or what did you want to be when you grew up? A scientist

2 What or who was your first obsession? Football

3 Who was your childhood hero (or is now)? Childhood hero is actually Einstein (yes, I know that is geeky)

4 What's your secret? Cannot sing or swim

5 *Star Trek* or *Star Wars*? Yep, *Star Wars*

6 Did any book change your life? If so, what was it? No, not yet

7 Favorite movie: *The Usual Suspects*

8 If you could hear only one piece of music again, what would it be? *Hotel California* (The Eagles)

9 Vinyl, cassette, 8-track, CD, MP3, or streaming? MP3

10 What do you prefer: Skype conference call or face-to-face meeting? Face-to-face

11 Your favorite ARM product is: iPhone

12 The best use of an ARM product is: In a smartphone

13 The best use of an ARM product would be ... The processors in the cloud somewhere that will run our lives after everything is connected

14 If you could bring anything back from extinction, what would it be? None

15 Your favorite mode of transport is ... Driving

16 What future invention would you like to make (or witness)? A virtual brain in the cloud somewhere that will organize my entire life after I am senile

17 Ready, Aim, Fire, or Ready, Fire, Aim? Aim, Fire, then Aim and Fire again. If you have to get ready first, you are already too slow in today's world

18 If you could ask one question of anybody, what would it be and to whom?

19 When were you happiest? Making things happen

20 What makes you angry? Prejudice

21 What does love feel like? Warm and fuzzy

22 Bitcoin or dollars? Dollars

23 How much is enough? Enough is enough

24 What is your greatest achievement? Having helped many partners to go from nobody to sector leaders. That and convincing my family to move from California to Shanghai

25 Beach or adventure holiday? Beach, definitely

YEAR OF BIRTH 1967
COUNTRY OF BIRTH China
CITY OF RESIDENCE Shanghai
UNIVERSITY + DEGREE MSEE U Mich, MBA UC Berkeley
TENURE AT ARM 2004-

ARM Top US Patent Grants
1995-2014

Total Patents / **Name of Inventor(s)** (with years 1995–2014 labeled)

58 Richard Grisenthwaite

45 Stuart Biles

 37 David Flynn

 36 David Bull

 34 Andrew Rose

 33 Scott Becker

 32 Krisztian Flautner

 31 Jørn Nystad

 30 David Seal

 29 Andrew Swaine

 29 John Horley

 29 Simon Craske

 27 Michael Williams

 27 Danny Kershaw

 27 Dominic Symes

 26 Chris Hinds

 26 Simon Ford

 25 David Mansell

 24 Simon Watt

 24 Paul Kimelman

23 Bruce Mathewson

 22 Stephen Hill

 22 Nicolas Chaussade

 22 David Jaggar

 22 Marlin Frederick, Jr.

 21 David Lutz

 21 Shidhartha Das

ARM **25**

84

Details of the ARM10 were first shown at Hot Chips in October 1998, adding new instructions in ARMv5 and a six-stage pipeline for higher-speed processing at 400 MHz and above, as well as a new vector floating point unit. But the silicon would take another 18 months to emerge from Lucent Technologies.

Powered by the supercharged share price, ARM's first full acquisition of another company was of Micrologic, a software house in Cambridge. The deal, led by vice president for operations Warren East, was for just £1.1 million. For comparison, during 1999 Broadcom bought five companies for a total of nearly $1 billion.

The same year, ARM's share price continued to grow, and it entered the FTSE100. Fourteen partners, including global names such as Qualcomm, IBM and Philips, had joined the partnership, which was now shipping over 50 million units per year. Coming full circle, Acorn ceased to trade and its holding in ARM shares was distributed to its shareholders. Acorn's set-top box business was sold off to Pace in Yorkshire; while the rump of the digital signal processing business, including chief architect Sophie Wilson, was sold to the managing director Stan Boland. This became Element 14 (after the chemical symbol for Silicon), and was sold to Broadcom the following year for $640 million. The rest of the value of Acorn was returned to shareholders as ARM shares.

The sale of ARM shares also reduced the board positions of Apple, opening up a space on the board, filled by Doug Dunn. GEC Plessey Semiconductors had been sold to Canadian chip designer Mitel Semiconductor in 1998, while in 1999 GEC bought networking companies Reltec and Fore Systems, renaming itself Marconi to cash in (it hoped) on the growing Internet bubble.

The last year of the 20th century saw the launch of a synthesizable version of the ARM9, which opened up more opportunities; the family would be a workhorse even more popular than the ARM7. It would be designed into chips for the Nintendo DS, Atheros Wi-Fi and TI's OMAP1. Eventually it would sell to over 250 licensees, including more than 100 licenses for the synthesizable ARM926EJ-S alone.

The semiconductor world had changed considerably in the years since ARM was launched. 172 million processors had been shipped by its partners by the end of the decade, and it employed over 400 staff in offices around the world, from Tokyo to Austin. The Cambridge campus was being expanded, and by November 1999 a whole new main building was ready for occupation on the Fulbourn Road site. Not that anyone was willing to move into it at the time — like the rest of the world, ARM held its breath waiting for the new millennium and the much-vaunted Year 2000 apocalypse. ▊

ABOVE   ARM CEO Robin Saxby launched a PR blitz in the run-up to, and in the wake of, the company's public listing.

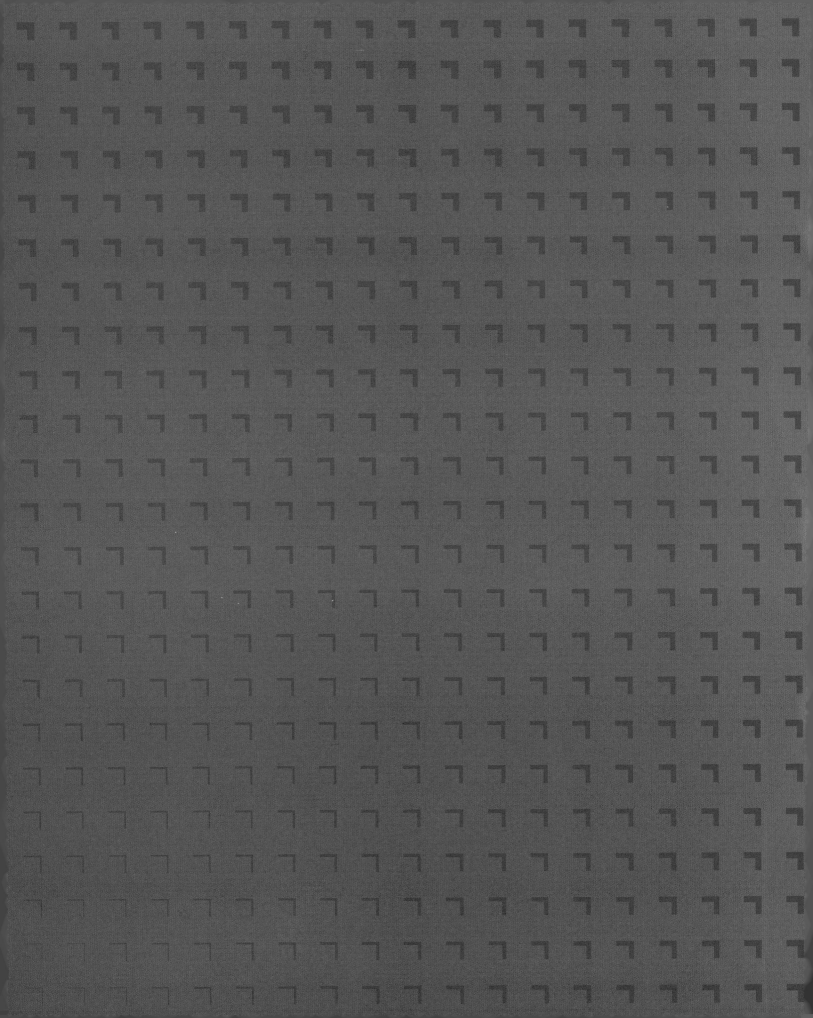

Chapter 3

May the Force be With You

The turn of the millennium was a disappointment for those expecting global Armageddon and the collapse of the world's technical infrastructure. Everybody was afraid that the Year 2000 (Y2K) "bug" was going to crash computer-controlled systems (in which the date was stored as only two decimal points) and bring chaos ... It didn't, of course. Not that anyone was taking any chances, especially at ARM where they discovered early in 1999 that only 30 percent of their systems were Y2K compliant. If the workstations and servers went down the company couldn't operate. So, despite their brand new building — ARM1 — being completed by the end of 1999 and it being as secure, up-to-date and as Y2K compliant as possible, they waited until after the turn of the year to move in — just in case. The 1998 share flotation and the coming of the millennium had, naturally, caused some people at ARM to re-evaluate their priorities. After the acquisition of three companies, the workforce comprised almost 700 people in offices around the world, and along with the growth came changes in the culture of the business.

It was a time of reflection for many people, and that bright ARM star Dave Jaggar, for one, decided to change his life radically. He cashed in his shares at what turned out to be the peak of the market, and returned to New Zealand. He continued to consult for ARM, but naturally became less involved in the business of day-to-day product development.

The company was flying, though. During the first year of the 21st century, ARM signed up eight new licensees, including field programmable chip designer Altera, who put ARM cores alongside its programmable fabric for their Excalibur family. In November 2000, just after the deal went through, John Daane took over as CEO at Altera, joining from LSI Logic. Other licensees included test equipment maker Agilent, German chip designer Micronas, Japanese chip giant Mitsubishi — which dominated the 4-bit and 8-bit microcontroller sector — plus Sanyo, Triscend and ZTEIC.

Not that life as a fast-growing company was without its hiccups. In March ARM had become involved in its first major legal battle when a startup called picoTurbo in Milpitas, California, developed a synthesizable processor that ran the same instructions as the ARM7TDMI. Set up in 1998 by Hong-Yi Chen, a chip architect from Sun Microsystems, and Peter Song, an engineer who had worked at Samsung and on AMD's

LEFT The Nintendo Game Boy Advance was launched in 2001 with a 3- by 2-inch color LCD screen and an ARM7TDI CPU. It sold over 81 million units worldwide.

25×25 Philip Davis

YEAR OF BIRTH 1966

COUNTRY OF BIRTH UK

CITY OF RESIDENCE Newbury BERKS

UNIVERSITY + DEGREE Cambridge, History/Theology

TENURE AT ARM 2014-

1 Who or what did you want to be when you grew up? When I was seven I wanted to be a boxer, to my mother's dismay, because of Muhammad Ali.

2 What or who was your first obsession? Football, and football stickers in the '70s (if anyone has '77/78 season Stan Bowles, QPR legend ...)

3 Who was your childhood hero (or is now)? Roy of the Rovers. I'm through that phase now.

4 What's your secret? I nearly became a Church of England minister before deciding on a career as a lawyer.

5 *Star Trek* or *Star Wars*? Keep it quiet but I've never been into either ...

6 Did any book change your life? If so, what was it? The Bible.

7 Favorite movie: *Local Hero* (1983) (directed by Bill Forsyth)

8 If you could hear only one piece of music again, what would it be? Bach's B minor Mass. Surely the greatest work ever composed — and one of the longest. I'd get over two hours to enjoy it.

9 Vinyl, cassette, 8-track, CD, MP3, or streaming? I have a loft full of vinyl but it doesn't get out much, so MP3.

10 What do you prefer: Skype conference call or face-to-face meeting? Skype is pretty amazing and all that, but given the choice, who doesn't prefer face to face?

11 Your favorite ARM product is: ARM7TDMi. Guy Larri, who's now in the legal group, holds the last patent covering that classic ARM product. We're proud of that in the legal team.

12 The best use of an ARM product is: Using MBED OS and device server to optimize eel farming.

13 The best use of an ARM product would be ... At the ALC 2015 I was in a syndicate group that envisaged ARM-powered smart bees. You heard it here first.

14 If you could bring anything back from extinction, what would it be? Let me come back on that ...

15 Your favorite mode of transport is ... Can't beat walking.

16 What future invention would you like to make (or witness)? I like the idea of witnessing eternity. I'd also like to invent a remote which switches off all screens in my house instantly and gets each of my kids to read a book — one part of that's easier than the other, I think.

17 Ready, Aim, Fire, or Ready, Fire, Aim? With an eye on the liability situation I prefer to take aim first.

18 If you could ask one question of anybody, what would it be and to whom? As a *Hitchiker's Guide to the Galaxy* fan (the original radio series) it would have to be — addressed to the supercomputer Deep Thought, of course — 'if the answer to the ultimate question is 42, what's the question?'

19 When were you happiest? Other than my wedding day, when playing cricket in the garden with my sons or getting a long hug from my daughter.

20 What makes you angry? I go all Victor Meldrew if I see anyone deliberately drop litter.

21 What does love feel like? Like life the way it was meant to be.

22 Bitcoin or dollars? That's very kind. Dollars please.

23 How much is enough? Whatever you've got.

24 What is your greatest achievement? Persuading my wife to marry me.

25 Beach or adventure holiday? Really don't mind if the right people are there too.

29000 RISC processor, picoTurbo believed it had implemented the v4T instruction set in a new way that it could sell to customers.

They showed ARM the design of the two processors they were working on, and ARM launched a lawsuit claiming that picoTurbo had infringed two of ARM's patents, particularly Dave Jaggar's technique for Thumb. No longer was ARM the plucky underdog with a new technology in the developing fabless industry — now it was the market leader and had a position to defend. The unfortunate situation mirrored that of MIPS Technologies, recently spun out from parent Silicon Graphics, where a startup called Lexra had developed an alternative implementation, or clone, in 1998. That dispute rumbled on for years until Lexra closed in 2003. The picoTurbo lawsuit would run for many months, widening to include claims on a total of seven patents. The claim was finally settled out of court in December 2001, but it marked another change for ARM. Robin had been vigorous about defending the case, and picoTurbo's accusations of bullying did not sit well with the company culture.

At the same time, ARM made moves toward a new digital industry, albeit one that had been under development almost from the very start: security. Smartcards and SIMs had huge potential for ARM, since millions of smartcards would soon be in use as payment cards, digital TV enablers and SIM cards in phones. Somewhat paradoxically, the growth of the security market was set against a backdrop of worry and fear on the stock markets. Although not apparent at the time, the Nasdaq had peaked on March 10, 2000. From then on it was all downhill, and tech companies suffered the fastest and greatest decline in values. Over the next two years more than $5 trillion would be wiped off the value of shares. As a relatively small company, the downturn in tech share prices was naturally worrying for ARM. The fundamental trends toward more automation, more electronics and more sophisticated processors for consumer and industry markets hadn't changed, but surviving the downturn would be a challenge. Partly because Robin had seen the industry regularly suffer cycles of ups and downs before, ARM had been, and continued to be, selective in its acquisitions. It invested $2 million in a Dublin-based chip design group called Parthus Technologies, whose 300 engineers were developing GPS navigation chips as well as Wi-Fi and cellular phone designs. There was a close connection between the companies: Kevin Fielding, the chief operating officer of Parthus, was the founder and managing director of the StrongARM group at Digital, and a key ARM supporter.

Parthus would later merge in 2002 with the US DSP group and Israeli chip designer Ceva to become ParthusCeva. During 2000 ARM used its still-buoyant, though declining, share price to buy three smallish companies: EuroMIPS Systems, Allant Software and Infinite Designs. Allant comprised five engineers in Walnut Creek, California, who developed design tools; EuropeMIPS employed 14 people in Sophia Antipolis in the south of France, where it was developing smartcard designs for e-commerce. The founder, Pascal Peru, had previously worked at the large Texas Instruments plant in the town, and would go on to run ARM France and the graphics business. The new Sophia team created the SecurCore family; their SC100, released in 2001, added security to the heart of processor. It was a key requirement in limiting the ways that the chip might be hacked. At the time, Java was becoming a serious language for the development of mobile applications — even SIM cards were beginning to use Sun's Java programming language. So ARM created a Java acceleration by putting Jazelle into the ARMv5TEJ architecture. Launched in October 2000, the first processor with Jazelle technology was the synthesizable ARM926EJ-S core. Despite its slow

ABOVE   The Nokia 7650, powered by the ARM926EJS, was the first Nokia phone to include picture messaging, a built-in camera and to be built on the Symbian OS.

start, ARM security technology became the industry standard, with the top 10 largest smartcard chip suppliers as licensees and key contributors to the billions of ARM cores that were shipped.

The Infinite Designs deal, led by Warren, saw the opening of ARM's Sheffield office, with nine employees. Set up by Jonathan Morris, Infinite Designs had been working with the AMBA technology to build system-on-chip devices, and would go on to lead the PrimeXsys development.

The management at the top of ARM was also shifting. Jamie switched from being chief operating officer to become chief strategy officer, and was replaced by Warren as COO. As business conditions became tougher the company limited the number of new additions to its payroll to a maximum of 150 people. But despite the challenging environment, the company ended the year on a high, with the licensing of one of its great competitors: Motorola Semiconductor. Hector Ruiz had left to run x86 chip designer AMD, and Fred Shlapak had taken over, opening up the chance for ARM cores to be used at the low end, with Motorola's own PowerPC cores embedded in higher

RIGHT ARM management team and founders, photoshopped into the ARM Cambridge staircase for a press picture.

ARM926EJS

DATE   September 2001

TECHNOLOGY   180 nm

TRANSISTORS   2,964K (896K Logic, 2,068K memories for 16 + 16 KB caches)

SIZE   8.98 mm^2 with 16 + 16 KB caches

FREQUENCY   200 MHz

POWER   1.49 mW/MHz

ARCHITECTURE   ARMv5

DESCRIPTION   The first synthesizable ARM application processor

25×25 Chris Kennedy

YEAR OF BIRTH 1964

COUNTRY OF BIRTH Manchester

CITY OF RESIDENCE London

UNIVERSITY + DEGREE Jesus, Cambridge. Pt 1 Engineering, Pt 2 Electrical Sciences

TENURE AT ARM 2015-

1 Who or what did you want to be when you grew up? Hoss (from Bonanza, a naff sixties cowboy serial)

2 What or who was your first obsession? Paddington. Including a refusal to eat anything that wasn't a marmalade sandwich

3 Who was your childhood hero (or is now)? I've never had a hero

4 What's your secret? It wouldn't be one if I told you

5 Star Trek or Star Wars? *Trek* but only the original. Spinoffs don't count

6 Did any book change your life? If so, what was it? *Last Chance to See* (1990), Douglas Adams

7 Favorite movie: *It's a Wonderful Life* (1946). Every Christmas

8 If you could hear only one piece of music again, what would it be? Beethoven's Pastoral Symphony

9 Vinyl, cassette, 8-track, CD, MP3, or streaming? Vinyl, cassette, aac, cd, Flac and streaming

10 What do you prefer: Skype conference call or face-to-face meeting? Face to face

11 Your favorite ARM product is: I don't have one yet

12 The best use of an ARM product is: Reducing man's footprint on earth

13 The best use of an ARM product would be ... Reducing man's footprint on earth

14 If you could bring anything back from extinction, what would it be? The slide rule

15 Your favorite mode of transport is ... Bicycle

16 What future invention would you like to make (or witness)? Teleportation. I hate the wasted time. But not to the wilderness; that has to be earned

17 Ready, Aim, Fire, or Ready, Fire, Aim? Ready, aim, wipe the sweat from my forehead, aim again and fire

18 If you could ask one question of anybody, what would it be and to whom? Neil Armstrong: 'How did it feel when you stepped out?'

19 When were you happiest? It's a tie. Birth of my first child and driving through the snow line into Meribel on a beautiful November day knowing I was going to ski until April

20 What makes you angry? Selfishness

21 What does love feel like? Warm, secure and safe

22 Bitcoin or dollars? Dollars (US of course)

23 How much is enough? Enough. You know it when you see it

24 What is your greatest achievement? Making it to 50 without screwing up too much

25 Beach or adventure holiday? Adventure, preferably near or on a beach

performance chips. "Motorola is a very significant ARM licensee," said Robin at the time, with considerable understatement.

PowerPC was more of a competitor to MIPS than ARM, but the deal proved to be the beginning of the end for Motorola's in-house Mcore low power RISC core, and an acknowledgement of ARM's increasing penetration into the chips for mobile phones market, where Motorola was a leading player. While this was seen at the time as protecting the Palm business that was moving to ARM, there was also an awareness that the 32-bit technology was increasingly moving into industrial applications and that a lower-cost approach was needed. "The embedded market is exploding — it's bigger than we expected," said Billy Edwards, senior vice president of Motorola's Semiconductor Products Sector. "This is a great combination that allows us to increase our embedded portfolio to suit everyone's needs."

The deal announced in December 2000 included one of those rare architecture licenses that allowed Motorola to run its own developments and enhance the implementations if it desired. This put it alongside Intel as the other architectural licensee with the StrongARM developments rebranded as Xscale. The move also saw engineers from Mcore, based in Austin, move across town to Intel's Xscale operation.

By the end of the year ARM had registered £100 million in revenues for the first

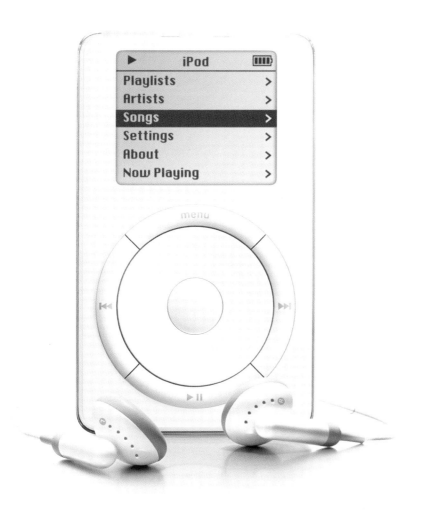

LEFT   The first-generation Apple iPod of 2001 used two ARM7TDI CPUs running at 90 MHz.

ARM Revenue **1991-2014**

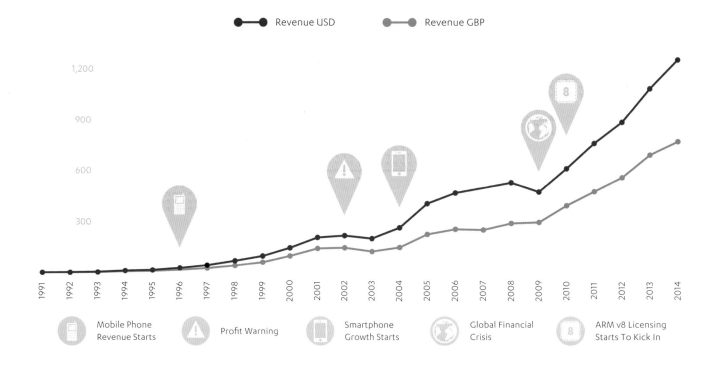

● — Revenue USD   ● — Revenue GBP

- 📱 Mobile Phone Revenue Starts
- ⚠ Profit Warning
- 📱 Smartphone Growth Starts
- 🌐 Global Financial Crisis
- 8 ARM v8 Licensing Starts To Kick In

time, with 50 licensees and over 400 million chips powered by ARM technology; 10 ARM-powered chips were being shipped every second. New sales offices opened in Taiwan, Israel and San Diego to support new customers, among them Qualcomm. There was also expansion for the emerging foundry side of the business. Taiwan Semiconductor Manufacturing Company and United Microelectronics Corporation became members of the ARM Foundry Program, which allowed them to sell cores to their customers, avoiding the need for a large upfront license fee but still providing the royalties. ARM became secure enough to look to the expansion and growth of the ARM architecture, not just the cash flow.

The following year would turn out to be momentous in many ways, with ARM's management changes, and drama in the wider world too, as the Internet bubble burst, share prices collapsed and global uncertainty increased. But ARM's share of the 32-bit embedded RISC microprocessor market was at 76.8 percent, which was a vindication of the strategy to become the global RISC standard. It had seen off PowerPC, SPARC and the other architectures on its way to lead in mobile phones, portable music systems, disk drive controllers and many other areas. It hadn't really made it on to the desktop, though, despite Intel's Xscale chip developments and Microsoft's PocketPC software. Nor had it made much of a dent in 4-bit and 8-bit controllers in washing machines and other home appliances. The ARM9EJ-S was an immediate success, with several companies adopting it for their chip designs. ARM made further small business deals, including the acquisition in February 2001 of key technologies and a 10-person embedded debug design team from Noral Micrologics in Blackburn, in the UK northwest.

ARM1176JZF-S

DATE	July 2004 EAC release
TECHNOLOGY	130 nm (first samples)
TRANSISTORS	~450 kgates excluding RAMs
SIZE	7.4 mm^2 with 16 + 16 KB L1 caches
FREQUENCY	370 MHz
POWER	1.2 mW/MHz
ARCHITECTURE	ARMv6 with TrustZone extensions
µARCHITECTURE	8-stage single issue pipeline with a branch predictor and optional vector floating point coprocessor
DESCRIPTION	The first ARM processor to implement TrustZone, AMBA AXI and IEM

Yet Robin's entrepreneurial "just do it" approach did not necessarily sit well with the merchant banks and the City of London traders in the shares of publicly listed companies. Sales of ARM licenses were slowing as customers became less certain about the future; the growth of royalties began to slow, too. At listed companies suffering such apparent slowdowns in growth the chief executive is usually replaced. The big question at ARM was: Who would replace Robin? The options were almost the same as back in 1991: Jamie, Mike and Tudor, for instance. But none of them had wanted it back then, plus they didn't have the experience of running a £100 million company with 700 employees. Of course, Jamie's previous role had been chief operating officer; his replacement, Warren, had also negotiated several recent acquisitions and thus become visible to the market; Simon Segars, meanwhile, was still gaining experience. Having an orderly transition was important, not least because when founders hand over, all too often unforeseen repercussions can result.

Then came the terrible events of September 11, 2001. The consequences of the attack on the World Trade Center in New York hit the US and global markets hard. When all flights to and from the US and many other major cities were grounded for several days, the world's traveling businesspeople were stranded in hotel rooms, working with laptop computers and telephones, watching in horror as the full extent of the catastrophic terrorist attack hit home. That tragic day played a significant part in tipping the global economy into the recession that had been approaching.

Nonetheless, in October 2001, Robin handed over to Warren and took on the role of executive chairman. Warren continued with the chief operating officer role for the day-to-day running of the company, while Robin stepped back. Mike Muller came on to the board as chief technology officer, Tudor took over as chief operating officer, and Jamie left the board. At the same time Tim O'Donnell stepped down as head of the US operation, to be replaced by Reynette Au. She had worked at AMD, Hobbit-designer AT&T Microelectronics and IBM; she was a highly experienced executive. Meanwhile, the company launched ARMv6 and the next generation of cores. ARMv6 added SIMD (Single Instruction, Multiple Data) processing to the architecture. This acknowledged the increasing importance of video and audio applications so that one instruction could be used on several blocks of data at the same time, doubling the performance of some critical tasks. The first core to use the new architecture would be the ARM1136 the following year, supporting up to eight pipeline stages rather than the six in the ARM926, and 64-bit data paths also helped get more performance. The core remains in use today in the Raspberry Pi low cost computer. But this would mark the last of the traditional ARM architectures, and a new approach was being developed.

Alongside the processor cores there was more focus on licensing "non-core-based" technology at ARM, such as peripheral blocks, models and application software. This grew to become over 10 percent of the total license revenues, driven by the PrimeCell peripherals and AMBA bus products. Sixteen different PrimeCell blocks had already been launched, with five more in development. These were being combined in an open platform to enable licensees to develop their own wireless solutions: PrimeXsys.

Another significant introduction in October 2001 was Apple's first-generation iPod. It wasn't the first MP3 music player, but its sizable hard drive gave the listener the opportunity to carry their whole music collection around for the first time. Two ARM cores made this happen, one for the hard drive controller and the other for the system control. The iPod would sell millions of units, and be a core platform for the later iPhone. As the first units shipped in the November it became increasingly clear

to people at ARM that they needed to keep their rapidly growing family of licensees happy and working with them.

In the early days, part of the licensee-relations management involved inviting ARM's six or eight customers to an annual gathering of partners in Cambridge. As a nod toward the university's May Ball tradition an event was usually hosted in the grounds of one of the historic colleges. ARM evangelists from the licensee companies always enjoyed visiting the city. As the company grew, though, it seemed useful and sensible to invite potential new supporters and suppliers of end equipment to the show. But with 50 licensees by the end of 2000, and a much wider range of applications, the once-intimate gathering had come to involve hundreds of people. It was still held at a college and managed to retain the feel of a "family affair," but it was clear that not every representative from important licensees could be entertained on a personal basis by the ARM management team. In order to maintain close contact with partners, the ARM Connected Community was launched to formalize the way partners and customers could use the ARM technology.

Managing customers and maintaining growth was now the primary concern of the new CEO, Warren East. At the end of what had proven to be a sober year he made changes to the company's senior management. Jonathan Brooks moved on as finance director, to be replaced by Tim Score from the privately funded software company Rebus Group. Naturally the news made the financial pages of the British newspapers, who described the switch as part of a "seven-year itch," and linked it to the fall of the

ABOVE   Two of the four Facebook founders Dustin Moskovitz (left) and Mark Zuckerberg at Harvard, 2004. They were taking the semester off to develop the social media site they'd launched only nine months earlier. It would help to revolutionize Internet use, moving people away from static computers to mobile technology.

YEAR OF BIRTH 1965

COUNTRY OF BIRTH Wales

CITY OF RESIDENCE Marlborough

UNIVERSITY + DEGREE BEng (Hons) Middlesbrough, MSc Durham University

TENURE AT ARM 2005-

25 × 25 Ian Drew

1 Who or what did you want to be when you grew up? Virgil Tracy (Thunderbird 2 pilot) or a rugby player

2 What or who was your first obsession? Rugby

3 Who was your childhood hero (or is now)? Nye Bevan or J. P. R. Williams. Being in a Welsh household they were two heroes

4 What's your secret? I played semi-pro basketball at college

5 *Star Trek* or *Star Wars*? *Star Wars*

6 Did any book change your life? If so, what was it? *A Brief History of Time* (1988), Stephen Hawking, as it re-ignited my love of physics; and *Huff the Hedgehog* (1966), Ruth Ainsworth, as it taught me to read

7 Favorite movie: *The Graduate* (1967). I love the music

8 If you could hear only one piece of music again, what would it be? *Tubular Bells* (1973), Mike Oldfield; great thinking music

9 Vinyl, cassette, 8-track, CD, MP3, or streaming? Vinyl, silly question

10 What do you prefer: Skype conference call or face-to-face meeting? Face to face

11 Your favorite ARM product is: ARM7tdmi, will still be being in production in 30 years

12 The best use of an ARM product is: Any tablet, it brought more of the Internet to the world than any other product

13 The best use of an ARM product would be ... A Mike Muller lookalike Barbie doll

14 If you could bring anything back from extinction, what would it be? My aunt

15 Your favorite mode of transport is ... My Land Rover Discovery — no technology but does exactly what I want

16 What future invention would you like to make (or witness)? Teleportation

17 Ready, Aim, Fire, or Ready, Fire, Aim? Ready fire aim

18 If you could ask one question of anybody, what would it be and to whom? Hitler ... why?

19 When were you happiest? Aged 19 and at college. I try and be 19 forever, for good or bad

20 What makes you angry? People not listening

21 What does love feel like? Family

22 Bitcoin or dollars? Dollars

23 How much is enough? When everyone has enough

24 What is your greatest achievement? My two daughters and being with my wife since school are equal

25 Beach or adventure holiday? Beach

share price from the heady heights of £10 to just under £4.

Not that Jonathan was willing to comply with that view. "ARM's a fantastic company but I wanted to do something different," he told the Daily Telegraph, adding: "Fortunately, because of that success I can afford to take a bit of time out and decide my next move. I don't want to be a chief executive or finance director of another big quoted company, though." The end-of-year results revealed that ARM was enjoying a healthy £146 million revenue, and had 77 partners. They offered a much-needed confidence boost to shareholders that the company could weather the coming storm.

The year 2002 proved to be both difficult and momentous for ARM. Q3 of the year was the first time the company missed financial analyst expectations. The share price plummeted, followed by the trauma of redundancies — for the first time ever. It wasn't an easy time for anyone at the company.

Nonetheless, ARM were gaining access to and making deals with its competitors' customers, shipping a billion ARM chips in just 10 years of existence. ARM made real inroads into areas previously dominated by MIPS or companies who had previously adhered to a "Not Invented Here" policy. Marvell, which grew rapidly via its own technologies using the fabless model, bought an ARM license in 2001; subsequently previously MIPS-based customers Broadcom and Philips both took licenses. They joined Matsushita, Micrel, eSilicon, Chip Express and ITRI as new licensees in 2002, three of which were focused on Microsoft Windows CE for portable computers. Intel launched its entry-level Xscale PXA250 processor, based on the StrongARMv5 architecture, for mobile computers and cellphones. The PXA260 would be released the following year, and a big revision codenamed Bulverde, the PXA270, unveiled in 2004 and was designed into the Palm Treo and Motorola Q smartphones.

However, the design team behind StrongARM moved from Intel in 2003 to set up PA Semi (previously Palo Alto Semiconductor) under Dan Dobberpuhl. His team was developing a power-efficient version of the PowerPC processors called the PA6T, and was financially backed by Texas Instruments, among others. If the first PA Semi power architecture processors (called PWRficient) chips, set to launch by the end of 2007, were adopted by powerful licensees, they could prove a significant competitor to ARM.

The same year, though, also saw Flextronics become the first ARM Licensing Partner program member. Flextronics was a contract equipment manufacturer that started out building designs such as phones or network switches for its customers. Increasingly it was designing the equipment and even the chips, so the licensing partner program allowed it to sublicense the ARM technology to its own customers.

The first implementations of the ARM11 microarchitecture, unlike the ARM10, were well received, and the company launched its development tools as a separate brand called RealView. At the same time the company was changing. Jamie resigned to join UK venture capital firm Pond Ventures, and Pete Magowan resigned to join another venture firm, Alta Berkeley. Other than Tim O'Donnell and Jonathan Brooks, these were the first senior executives to leave, and the first of the founders. At the same time, Reynette left to join Triscend, which was developing a competing processor based on Hitachi's SuperH RISC processor. Mike took over the running of marketing for a second time, albeit briefly, and hired Mike Inglis from a management consultancy firm. He'd previously worked at Texas Instruments at the same time as Warren.

Still, the billion shipments was a key milestone for the company, matching Intel's 1 billion PC chips shipped that same year. But this was just the start — the road to 10 billion and 50 billion would prove to be much quicker.

Director and Company Secretary **Timeline**

ARM **25**

102

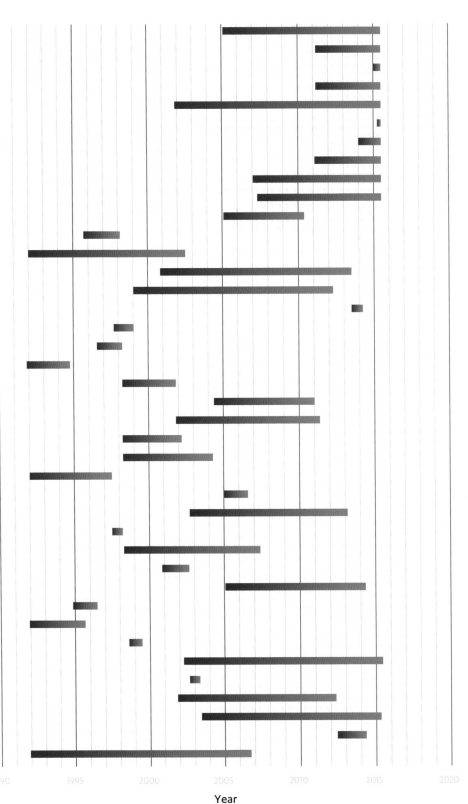

Simon Anthony Segars
Andrew James Green
John Yun Liu
Larry Hirst
Michael Peter Muller
Philip Stephen James Davis (co. sec)
Stuart John Chambers
Janice Mary Roberts
Kathleen Anne O'Donovan
Young Kwon Sohn
Dr Lucio Luidi Lanza
David Gordon Lee
David Nigel MacKay
David Warren Arthur East
Douglas John Dunn
Eric Meurice
Gary Joseph Wipfler
Georges Jean-Philippe Guyon De Chemilly
Giancarlo Zanni
James Stuart Urquhart
Jeremy Paul Scudamore
John Colbert Scarisbrick
Jonathan Brooks
Lawrence Gordon Tesler
Malcolm Graham Bird
Mark Rainold Templeton
Michael James Inglis
Peter Bondar
Peter Edward Blackburn Cawdron
Peter John Magowan
Philip Edward Rowley
Richard Ernest O Leary
Samuel Alan Wauchope
Stan Boland
Timothy Score
Timothy Score (co. sec)
William Tudor Brown
Patricia Mary Alsop (co. sec)
Sir John Gordon St Clair Buchanan
Sir Robin Keith Saxby

Year

Cortex-A8

DATE	July 2006: Cortex-A8 optimized EAC release and March 2007: first synthesized EAC release
TECHNOLOGY	65 nm
TRANSISTORS	420K (cell count)
SIZE	8.7 mm^2 (32 + 32 KB L1 and 256 KB L2 caches)
FREQUENCY	1 GHz
POWER	0.52 mW/MHz dynamic 520 mW @ 1 GHz
ARCHITECTURE	ARMv7-A: Thumb-2, NEON, VFPv3, TrustZone
μARCHITECTURE	Superscalar (dual-issue, in-order), 13-stage integer pipeline, integrated L2, 2.0 DMIP/MHz
DESCRIPTION	First superscalar and integrated L2 and NEON. Datapaths tiled or synthesized. Used in Apple A4 SOC, iPad-1

RIGHT   The first generation of iPhone 3G (2007), which used a Samsung-ARM1176JFS CPU. The iPhone 3GS (2009) and 4 (2010) used an ARM Cortex-A8 CPU, the 4S (2011) a dual core Cortex-A9.

In 2003, interest surged in the next generation of digital mobile phone technology: 3G. Symbian had developed the first mobile operating system designed specifically for ARM, which would drive further designs, while licensees STMicroelectronics, TI, ARM and Nokia set up the MIPI alliance for mobile application processors. That allowed a standard interface for the application processor, which was the main market for the ARM9 and the coming ARM11 devices. The Thumb instruction set was enhanced with 32-bit instructions, creating Thumb-2; and system cost was reduced with the ARMv6T2 architecture using 26 percent less memory than pure 32-bit code, while at the same time delivering 25 percent better performance than 16-bit code alone.

Warren took pains to make sure other areas of the business were not ignored. The company acquired Adelante Technologies, a developer in Belgium that had tools for high speed design optimization, and launched the CoreSight real-time debug and trace technology to help designers with the development of multicore systems. This was essential technology. Desktop chip makers were pushing higher clock speeds to get more performance but it was at the expense of more power. ARM had to take a different approach. Multiple cores could all run at a slower speed to do the same tasks with less power, but the problem was making them work in the design. The launch of AMBA 3.0 — AXI — was part of this, allowing the cores to be connected up more efficiently, as was a tie up with National Semiconductor to vary the clock frequency and voltage of the cores to match performance requirements.

Security was still a key area of development and design, and when TrustZone was launched in 2003 it embedded new security blocks deep into the processor. It allowed a "root of trust" so that the security already in smartcards and SIM cards could be built directly into a portable system via the application processor. Artisan Components in the US had been working increasingly closely with ARM, supplying leading-edge design blocks and technologies. At the time, Taiwan Semiconductor Manufacturing Company's 0.13-μm technology was being used by 200 customers, making 3,000 different products in its fabs, many of them powered by the ARM cores, and the 90-nm process technology was being tested. By the end of the year ARM would be building its reference platforms with Artisan's technology. It also successfully defended another patent case, this time brought against the company by Nazomi over the implementation of the Java Jazelle technology.

ARM's biggest acquisition deal happened in 2004, with the purchase of Artisan Components for $1 billion. It was an event that would both transform the company with a further shift away from Cambridge and bring continued scrutiny from the financial markets. The move was driven by a desire to go beyond the traditional business of licensing processor cores, and the ever-increasing importance of the quality of implementation of its architectures in meeting the needs of markets as diverse as low-cost sensors to high performance servers.

The acquisition followed the launch of a whole new architecture and naming scheme that marked a further departure from the original instruction set developed by Sophie Wilson and Steve Furber. The Cortex branding moved away from the ARM1 to ARM11 numbering system, and instead created three different families of cores with applications processors named Cortex-A, real-time Cortex-R and microcontrollers Cortex-M. The architecture was also re-designed to reflect the naming, with distinct profiles for each of the classes of processors. Support for the original 26-bit address was lost in ARMv4, but the biggest change was in the ARMv7-M profile, which further broke the link with the past by dropping support for the 32-bit instruction set and only ran Thumb/Thumb-2 code.

It was a key step for Mike Muller as chief technology officer. No longer could 32-bit ARM code from the 1990s be run on an ARM Cortex-M chip in 2004. But it signaled a significant investment in the embedded markets and the imminent rise of the Internet of Things. The story ARM told was that this didn't matter — the first core, the Cortex-M3, was aimed at the small microcontrollers in white goods, such as washing machines and toasters, that wouldn't be running old code anyway. As it was all supported by the development tools, and almost all the code was now written in the C programming language, it could easily be compiled to run on the new chips. The Cortex-M3 had its own architecture, the ARMv7-M, which allowed a low power, three-stage pipeline for those low-cost applications. Later versions added the signal processing SIMD instructions for the higher performance Cortex-M4 family with the v7E-M architecture, and cut out more of the 32-bit instructions for the even lower-cost Cortex-M0 with the v6-M architecture. "People said we were mad to do it, because ARM7 had that massive installed base," recalled Mike, talking to Chris Edwards for the Institution of Engineering and Technology magazine. "We agonized over it for a long time and, in the end, made the right choice because it opened up the microcontroller market. However, we understood that in other areas, you have to have 100 percent backward compatibility, so we maintained that for other processor cores."

The PrimeXsys platform, launched in 2002 around the ARM11, had not been so successful. "If I look at where it went wrong, it was ahead of its time," explained Mike. "We were building the same systems over and over again. We saw the same issues coming up, so why not standardize? Our lead partners said: 'We don't want to be

25 × 25 Tom Lantzsch

YEAR OF BIRTH   1960

COUNTRY OF BIRTH   USA

CITY OF RESIDENCE   Palo Alto

UNIVERSITY + DEGREE   BSEE
Michigan State, MS Finance
University of Texas (Dallas)

TENURE AT ARM
2006-

1 Who or what did you want to be when you grew up?   A CIA spy

2 What or who was your first obsession?   Things that went fast or just going fast

3 Who was your childhood hero (or is now)?   Jack Nicklaus

4 What's your secret?   I prefer quiet time alone vs time with a group

5 Star Trek or Star Wars?   Star Wars

6 Did any book change your life? If so, what was it?   No

7 Favorite movie: —

8 If you could hear only one piece of music again, what would it be?   Moby Dick (1969), Led Zeppelin

9 Vinyl, cassette, 8-track, CD, MP3, or streaming?   Vinyl

10 What do you prefer: Skype conference call or face-to-face meeting?   Face-to-face

11 Your favorite ARM product is: Current app processor in my phone

12 The best use of an ARM product is: Powering my smartphone

13 The best use of an ARM product would be ...   Creation of a transporter

14 If you could bring anything back from extinction, what would it be?   —

15 Your favorite mode of transport is ...   Bike

16 What future invention would you like to make (or witness)?   An instant transporter

17 Ready, Aim, Fire, or Ready, Fire, Aim?   Ready Aim Fire

18 If you could ask one question of anybody, what would it be and to whom?   —

19 When were you happiest?   My high school years in the summer

20 What makes you angry?   Poor time management that creates 'urgencies' on me

21 What does love feel like?   —

22 Bitcoin or dollars?   Bitcoin

23 How much is enough?   When you have the financial freedom to pursue your passion

24 What is your greatest achievement?   My children

25 Beach or adventure holiday?   Adventure

standardized, we want to differentiate.' You can't expect all your initiatives to be successful all the time," he continued. "As with all your failures, you learn a bit about why you went wrong and how you could do better. Now we have an even broader community involved in the activity, but we understand better how to support the needs of the early adopters and later licensees — and everyone is more aware of the cost of differentiation on our software community — and when they will see benefits. That's what we learned from the PrimeXsys engagement."

That didn't stop other technologies being introduced with varying degrees of success. NEON provided additional media acceleration performance in a block that could be added to an existing processor, while OptimoDE added signal processing accelerators from the Adelante acquisition. The OptimoDE Data Engine cores employ a "very long instruction word" (VLIW)–style architecture where the data path is entirely user defined so that it can be optimized to the particular application. Typical instruction lengths varied between 16 and 256 bits, and the size and type of local storage and interconnect were also fully configurable.

Simultaneously the MPCore multiprocessor, the first integrated multiprocessor to boost performance and keep power consumption down, was launched. The company acquired Axys Design Automation to help design, model and simulate these complex systems at a higher level with System C. There were other complex business deals being done, too. ARM didn't have leading-edge graphics technology, so it sublicensed Imagination Technology's PowerVR graphics. This had been used in Sega's Dreamcast console, and was a highly power-efficient architecture. Samsung licensed the PowerVR MBX technology from ARM for chips that would ultimately be used by ARM's founding shareholder, Apple.

Another 65 licenses were signed with more companies, including Aplix, Atheros, Kawasaki, NEC, Socle, Sony Ericsson, Thomson, Toshiba, Samsung and ZRRT — and neighbor Cambridge Silicon Radio, to replace their 16-bit XAP processor. ARM also signed up with a subsidiary of Philips called Handshake Solutions to develop a commercial clockless asynchronous core similar to the Amulet2 that Steve Furber had been working on at Manchester. The share price struggled along with the rest of the semiconductor industry, but revenue kept growing to £152 million.

In 2005, Simon Segars joined the board of ARM. At the time, WiMax was a hot topic, with Sequans collaborating with ARM on a reference design for the wireless local loop technology on what proved to be an unsuccessful attempt by Intel to undermine the strength of the cellular business. The drive at ARM on design tools continued, and a competitor — Keil Software — was added to the company. It gave ARM a set of tools for software developers which also supported other architectures, while ensuring that the latest ARM technology was always included. This became increasingly important with the launch of the first of the Cortex-A processors. The Cortex-A8 was the first high performance applications processor to really tap into the high-speed design techniques used by StrongARM to get to 1 GHz through its ARMv7-A architecture. It would be used by Qualcomm and Apple, but at this point, TI was the lead partner for its OMAP smartphone chips, with the core combining the Thumb-2 instructions set with NEON, Jazelle and TrustZone technologies.

"TI has been one of ARM's lead partners for more than 12 years, and during this time we have shipped an impressive 1.7 billion ARM processor-based chips," said Gilles Delfassy, TI's senior vice president of its Wireless Terminals Business Unit. "TI built the industry's leading baseband processing product and OMAP applications processor

ARM Cortex-M0

DATE	March 2009 EAC release
TECHNOLOGY	180 nm ultra-low-leakage
TRANSISTORS	~12K gates (minimum configuration)
SIZE	0.13 mm^2
FREQUENCY	50 MHz
POWER	64.3 uW/MHz
ARCHITECTURE	ARMv6-M
µARCHITECTURE	3-stage Thumb instructions only
DESCRIPTION	ARM's smallest CPU for low-cost microcontroller and mixed-signal applications.

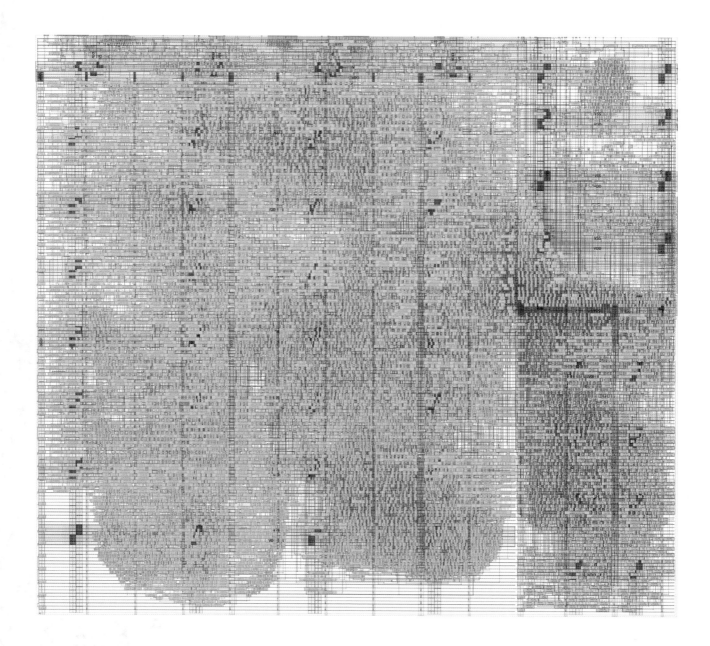

by combining ARM processors with TI DSPs for telecom and multimedia and by supporting microcomputing based on open standards. And now, as the first Cortex-A8 processor licensee, TI continues to be first to the market with the most advanced wireless processing solutions."

At the other end of the scale, the DesignStart Program brought together all the processor core, interconnect and peripheral technologies from ARM, and combined them with the physical technologies from Artisan so that companies could easily use them at a wide range of foundries. This was a compelling step forward, replacing the need for different technologies from different providers for separate foundries. Instead, DesignStart made it easier for both the chip designers and the foundries to get the chips made.

The Artisan acquisition brought more US interest in ARM, and alongside companies such as Intel, TI and Sony, it was recognized at the end of 2005 by US publication Electronic Business as one of the 10 most significant companies in electronics over the past 30 years.

Growth had returned to ARM, which now had some 1300 staff around the world. Revenue was boosted to £232 million by the first full year following the Artisan deal. The company continued to expand, and 2006 saw Handshake Solutions launch its clockless ARM chip, and the board made a big move into graphics by acquiring Norwegian designer Falanx Microsystems. Its Mali graphics processors brought

ABOVE A bank of Samsung flat-screen TVs on display at a trade show in Berlin, 2008, all powered by ARM.

graphics technology into ARM for the first time, but precipitated a falling out with previous partner Imagination Technologies and its PowerVR graphics. Not everything went ARM's way. The Cortex-R4 real-time processor was slow to reach widespread adoption. Intended for 3G smartphone designs, it could also be used for hard-disk drives with tightly coupled memory for smaller and more efficient integration with rapid response times. However, the inclusion of memory protection and fault tolerances for safety-critical applications made it perfect for automotive designs, and found great success with TI, coming full circle to their original stated goal of 1993 in licensing ARM for automotive use. The Cortex-R4 slowly but surely became the mainstay of the real time product family.

Meanwhile, Intel sold its Xscale to Marvell Semiconductor for $600 million, and the StrongARM technology moved deeper into the embedded market. The year also saw the end of Robin's time at the company. In May 2006 he stepped down as chairman and was replaced by Doug Dunn. It was, as they say, the end of an era.

Not that it was the end of ARM's march toward global leadership. In 2007 over 5 billion ARM cores shipped, and the Cortex-M1 processor was launched, the first ARM processor designed specifically for use in field-programmable gate arrays such as those from Altera and Xilinx. The new Cortex-A9 processors, with a key multicore option, targeted scalable performance and low power designs for companies like NEC, NVIDIA and Renesas, while the SecurCore SC300 processor was launched for smartcards. But the biggest impact came with the launch of the iPhone.

Just as the iPod had driven up unit shipments, so the iPhone, with its ARM-based modem from Infineon and ARM-based applications processor made by Samsung, would drive more adoption of the technology. In just a year the number of ARM cores shipped jumped from 5 billion to 10 billion. In 2008, and just ahead of a particularly severe financial crisis, ARM supplied the cores in LG Viewty, Nokia N95 and Sony Ericsson P1i smartphones, in Garmin, Navman and TomTom navigation systems, in Sony

ABOVE   ARM Norway baked a cake in the shape of the Mali to celebrate the twentieth anniversary of the company's existence.

25 × 25 Pete Hutton

1 Who or what did you want to be when you grew up? Involved in the space program. It was all Apollo when I was a kid

2 What or who was your first obsession? Science fiction

3 Who was your childhood hero (or is now)? Neil Armstrong

4 What's your secret? Wouldn't you like to know …

5 *Star Trek* or *Star Wars*? *Trek*

6 Did any book change your life? If so, what was it? They all change my life, only the degree varies

7 Favorite movie: *Bladerunner* (1982)

8 If you could hear only one piece of music again, what would it be? My current favourite. It always changes

9 Vinyl, cassette, 8-track, CD, MP3, or streaming? MP3

10 What do you prefer: Skype conference call or face-to-face meeting? Face to face

11 Your favorite ARM product is: My current smartphone

12 The best use of an ARM product is: My current smartphone

13 The best use of an ARM product would be … So many, can't pick one

14 If you could bring anything back from extinction, what would it be? Mammoth

15 Your favorite mode of transport is … Cycle

16 What future invention would you like to make (or witness)? Teleportation, so I can spend less time on planes!

17 Ready, Aim, Fire, or Ready, Fire, Aim? Ready, Fire, Aim

18 If you could ask one question of anybody, what would it be and to whom? Karl Marx: 'Dude, why did you get it so badly wrong?'

19 When were you happiest? This weekend, at home with my family

20 What makes you angry? Irritated, lots of things; angry, not many. People who are only out for themselves would be one. Deliberate rudeness or lack of thought, another

21 What does love feel like? Overwhelming and necessary

22 Bitcoin or dollars? Dollars

23 How much is enough? When you don't need any more. Need being the operative word rather than want

24 What is your greatest achievement? My three kids, and staying married

25 Beach or adventure holiday? A mix of both

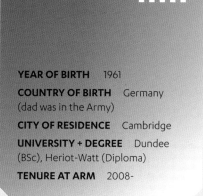

YEAR OF BIRTH 1961

COUNTRY OF BIRTH Germany (dad was in the Army)

CITY OF RESIDENCE Cambridge

UNIVERSITY + DEGREE Dundee (BSc), Heriot-Watt (Diploma)

TENURE AT ARM 2008-

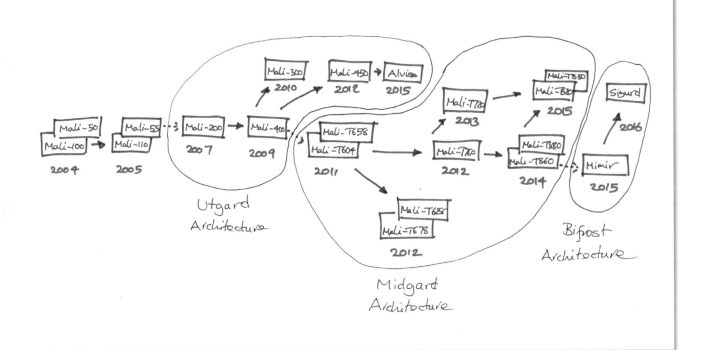

Mali-100 / Mali-50 — 2004
Mali-110 / Mali-55 — 2005
Mali-200 — 2007
Mali-400 — 2009
Mali-300 — 2010
Mali-450 — 2012 → Alvise — 2015

Utgard Architecture

Mali-T658 / Mali-T604 — 2011
Mali-T658 / Mali-T678 — 2012
Mali-T760 / Mali-T720 — 2012, 2013
Mali-T880 / Mali-T860 — 2014
Mali-T830 / Mali-T820 — 2015

Midgard Architecture

Sigurd — 2016
Mimir — 2015

Bifrost Architecture

RIGHT How the Mali chip evolved, as drawn by an engineer who knows ...

video cameras and the Nintendo DS handheld gaming device, as well as in Toshiba HD digital televisions, Samsung and Seagate hard disk drives, Bosch automotive braking systems, HP printers, and wireless routers from Linksys and Netgear. All the handsets for China's 3G cellular trials were ARM-based, and the Mali-200 graphics processor unit became fully integrated with the ARM cores thanks to the acquisition of Falanx. Apple's $278 million purchase of PA Semiconductor brought it the StrongARM team there. Although the buyout sparked rumors of an Apple move to the PowerPC, in fact the StrongARM experience came to good use on Apple's own ARM chips that would later be used in the iPad.

As the global financial meltdown gathered pace, ARM held a total of 587 licenses. Remarkably, they were still shipping the ARM7TDMI to new customers. The ARM926 was the best-selling core, but the ARM11 was catching up fast. The Cortex-A8 and Cortex-A9 were taking off with the smartphone makers, while the Cortex-M3 was slowly gaining traction as a microcontroller. The company continued to be flexible with business models, and the ARM IP Portfolio Program provided access to a comprehensive range of ARMIP quickly, via a design house. Socle Technology in Taiwan was the first to enroll, licensing the ARM11 family. Mali-200 and Mali-55 graphics cores, CoreSight (the new name for AMBA) and PrimeCell peripherals were adapted so that companies who were not chip specialists could still use ARM technology. Chartered Semiconductor Manufacturing, one of Taiwan Semiconductor Manufacturing Company's competitors, was a major shareholder in Socle, and sought to provide a "one-stop shop" solution in the latest manufacturing technology.

In 2009 a 2 GHz-capable Cortex-A9 dual core processor was implemented, and a Swedish video technology developer, Logipard, was acquired. But it was the Cortex-M0 that made the greatest impact. The Cortex-M0 broke the link with the 32-bit past. It no longer supported the 32-bit instructions in Thumb-2 to get smaller size, smaller code size and low power to replace the 8-bit and 16-bit devices. With 15 licensees in the first nine months of the year, the Cortex-M0 would prove to be the fastest-growing processor in the company's history. But the global recession resulting from the banking crisis continued to shake markets, undermine governments and throw currencies into a downward spiral. Although revenue dropped by 10 percent to £489 million, ARM remained confident that it could still take market share and grow the number of units shipped. It took encouragement in that belief from market research firm Semico, which finished the year with the prediction that by 2011 ARM would be the biggest microcontroller architecture, beating x86 and PowerPC.

World domination had been established — in the nicest possible way, of course. ∎

Chapter 6
To Infinity ...

n November 2010 every ARM colleague worldwide arrived at work and was given the future. Their future, ARM's future — everyone's future, even. It was right there in front of them, carefully and securely wrapped in a box the size of a large book (a bit like this one).

This gift of the future didn't make it into ARM's 2010 annual report. It was a gift from ARM itself, a celebration of its 20th anniversary — a significant milestone in the company's development. After a hard couple of years, ARM had finally and definitively emerged from the financial crisis of 2008-2009. As Ian Thornton, head of investor relations, put it, "Revenues took a bit of a curtsey, but we were nowhere near as affected as other companies."

On February 8, 2010, ARM had joined the UK's FTSE100, replacing chocolate-maker Cadbury. When first listed on the London Stock Exchange in 1998, ARM's revenues were £42.3 million and its profits £9.4 million. In 2010 its revenues would be almost ten times greater, at £406.6 million, and its profits increased seventeen-fold, to £164.3 million. By 2014, revenues would have almost doubled again, to £795.2 million, and profits more than doubled, to £400.3 million. Between 2010 and 2015, ARM would outperform the FTSE100 by 382 percent, excluding dividends.

That outperformance was driven, in good part, by the future as represented by the contents of that package on every ARM employee's desk: a first-generation iPad, safe in its own special custom case. At that moment, an iPad was, pretty much, the most exciting piece of tech even an ARM team member could wish to have. It was so new that there were not just countries but whole swathes of the world where it wouldn't be available for months.

In logistical terms, just getting them to people was quite something. The idea, the ordering and preparing, the whole process, everything had been done in almost complete secrecy. Only office managers knew it was coming. The packages had been delivered to ARM's offices worldwide. (Well, everyone except the team in the Taiwan office, where they got stuck in customs.)

The gift's significance, however, stretched way beyond excellent logistics. As well as bringing the future to the — actual, physical — hands of everyone at ARM, it also reached back, referentially, into the company's history. Though Apple disinvested in

LEFT   The iPad (launched 2010), made possible by ARM Cortex-A8 CPUs.

25 × 25 Andy Smith

YEAR OF BIRTH   1966
COUNTRY OF BIRTH   Ireland
CITY OF RESIDENCE   Cambridge
UNIVERSITY + DEGREE   Oxford:
Mathematics and Computer Science
TENURE AT ARM
2014-

1 Who or what did you want to be when you grew up?   Taller

2 What or who was your first obsession?   Football

3 Who was your childhood hero (or is now)?   Trevor Brooking and then Michael Jordan

4 What's your secret?   That information is classified

5 *Star Trek* or *Star Wars*?   *Star Trek*

6 Did any book change your life? If so, what was it?   *To Kill a Mockingbird* (1960), Harper Lee

7 Favorite movie: *Four Weddings and a Funeral* (1994)

8 If you could hear only one piece of music again, what would it be?   Verdi's *Requiem* (as performed by the Anchorage Concert Chorus in 1994)

9 Vinyl, cassette, 8-track, CD, MP3, or streaming?   Streaming

10 What do you prefer: Skype conference call or face-to-face meeting?   Face-to-face

11 Your favorite ARM product is: iPad

12 The best use of an ARM product is: Remote control for the world

13 The best use of an ARM product would be ...   To ensure your boss's technology never breaks and cause him to be grumpy

14 If you could bring anything back from extinction, what would it be?   The dinosaur

15 Your favorite mode of transport is ...   Bicycle

16 What future invention would you like to make (or witness)?   Time travel

17 Ready, Aim, Fire, or Ready, Fire, Aim?   Ready, Aim, Fire

18 If you could ask one question of anybody, what would it be and to whom?   Fermat — were you just having a joke with the whole margin thing?

19 When were you happiest?   After the birth of my two girls

20 What makes you angry?   Incorrect dishwasher stacking which is not space efficient

21 What does love feel like?   Soft and squishy

22 Bitcoin or dollars?   Dollars

23 How much is enough?   Siri says ... (a game show that aired on GSN in 2008)

24 What is your greatest achievement?   Answering these 25 questions

25 Beach or adventure holiday?   Adventure

ARM, gradually, in the late 1990s, the two companies remained closely linked. In 2013, online UK trade journal The Register described ARM as "the company that helped Steve Jobs save Cupertino from annihilation."

ARM enabled that rescue operation via what it has referred to as its world-leading and low-cost "energy-sipping processors." ARM's processors are architected for low power, efficient implementation and high code density. Which is why the ARM Cortex-A8 was at the heart and core of the iPhone 3GS, which launched in June 2009, two years after the first-generation iPhone, which went on sale the same year that work started on the ARMv8 architecture — which would eventually first ship in 2014, the year Forbes ranked ARM as the third most innovative company in the world.

The iPad had only been announced in early 2010, on January 27, by Steve Jobs, at a press conference in San Francisco. "A magical and revolutionary device at an unbelievable price," he said of Apple's latest innovation — 27 years after he first outlined a future that would arrive for everyone at ARM. In a 1983 speech at the International Design Conference in Aspen, the theme of which was "The Future Isn't What It Used To Be," the Apple CEO had shared his dream of "an incredibly great computer in a book that you can carry around with you and learn how to use in 20 minutes … with a radio link … to hook up to … databases and other computers." Whch, when you think about it, is an iPad by any other name.

The first iPads went on sale in the US on April 3, with prices starting at $499. A million were sold in the first month. On May 28, iPads were made available in the UK, Australia, Canada, France, Germany and Japan. On July 23, they reached Hong Kong,

ABOVE   The 20th anniversary of ARM was celebrated differently in offices around the world: in France they baked cakes, in India they danced, in China they posed in front of a wall, in the UK they drank beer, and in Korea (above) they said it with cartoons.

BELOW When the Samsung Galaxy SII was launched in 2011 it had more than 3 million preorders. One of the most popular touch-screen Android phones in the world, it uses an ARM Cortex-A9 CPU and ARM Mali-400 MP4 GPU.

Ireland, Mexico, New Zealand and Singapore. On September 17, mainland China. Across the world, 3 million were sold in its first 80 days on the market. In October, Jobs announced that iPads were outselling Macs.

No one can recall where the gift idea came from, but it was obviously the right thing to do, and Ian Drew made it all happen. He had come to ARM from Intel intending to change the industry in 2005. The decision to make the gift was agreed at a board meeting in the spring, because it would show ARM technology at its best. Within a couple of months the decison had an extra, beneficial effect because ARM people were using their tablets everywhere, in trains, in bed. It proved that what ARM was doing was right, that it was on to something.

Inside every last one of those millions of iPads was an efficient 1 GHz ARM Cortex-A8. As The Register commented the week before the iPad launch, it was "hard to imagine Apple using anything other than an ARM-based processor in there."

In 2010, ARM was fulfilling its own predictions of its future. In 1999, a year after its secondary listing on Nasdaq, the company published a forward-looking review. It considered, carefully, ARM's place in the next generation of digital electronic applications, seeing the company's opportunity in the sweet spot where communications and consumer electronics would converge. "This is our chosen area; this is where we are focused, and it is the area where we believe our future will be big. Really big," read the review. It dreamed of "entirely new and potentially huge markets" out there waiting to be brought to life on mobile devices. "Imagine arriving in a strange town for the first time, and finding the local hoteliers, retailers and other service providers. Instantly. You would never be lost again." TripAdvisor? Google maps?

On that November day in 2010 the future had arrived, then. Or was well on its way, at least. By the end of that year, 6.1 billion ARM processor-based chips shipped, which was a 56 percent increase on the previous year's total, more than 150 percent more than five years earlier and many million times more than in the first year ARM chips were shipped, in 1991. Between 2006 and 2010 ARM had more than doubled its share of both the hard disk drive and digital TV markets. Its market penetration of the microcontroller market increased tenfold. These chips, which are used in consumer products from washing machines to toys, are the ones at the base of the price pyramid — less than a dollar each. They have to be as cheap as, well, chips. But, of course, they still need to be smart.

As of 2010, more and more ARM chips were making their way into mobile phones. This was essentially a result of mobiles getting smarter. While a basic mobile would have just one chip, a typical smartphone would generally use three or four of them. These chips were also more expensive — and so generated higher revenue per phone. There were more of these chips, too. Mobile phone sales were increasing by an overall annual 20 percent — while that figure was 55 percent for smartphones. In 2009 the average number of ARM-based chips in a phone rose from 2.1 to 2.5. In its annual report for 2010 ARM predicted that, in the medium term, "we believe that we can grow our revenues at about twice the rate of our costs." And fourth-generation mobile phone networks were still only on their way around the world. Though introduced in South Korea as early as 2006, commercial 4G took time to become universal.

With hindsight it is clear that 2010 was a year in which boundaries between technologies began to slip. A new kind of mobile computing was emerging, of which the iPad was a harbinger. In ARM's own words, as stated in the year-end report, "Smartphones are getting smarter and laptops are getting smaller and more portable

Cortex-A9

DATE	March 2011 volume production
TECHNOLOGY	45 nm
TRANSISTORS	3.5M gates (dual A9 32k/32k + PL310 — no RAM)
SIZE	4.9 mm^2
FREQUENCY	up to 1.2 GHz
POWER	1.35 mW/Mhz
ARCHITECTURE	ARMv7-A
µARCHITECTURE	First OoO speculative CPU in ARM
DESCRIPTION	First large volume multicore

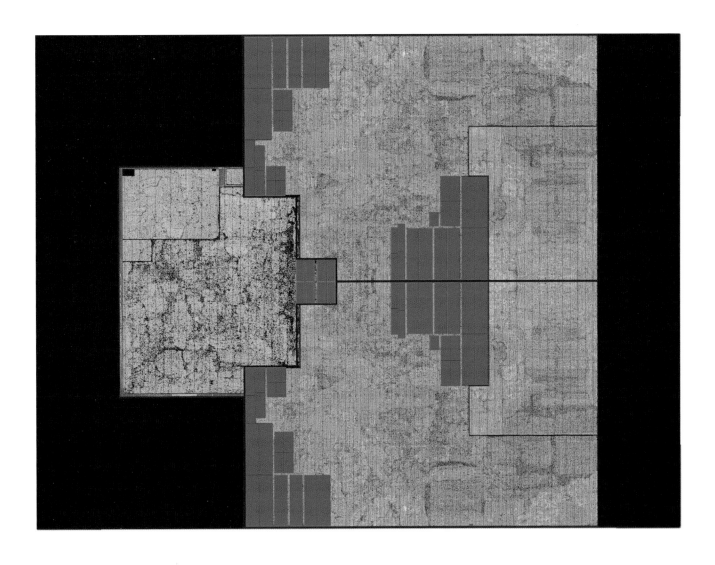

... creating an opportunity for smartphone technology to cross over into laptops and laptop technology to cross over into smartphones." Welcome to the future, the very one that dropped into ARM employees' hands in the November of 2010.

At the core of that future was something else from the past, something that had been there since the very beginning: ARM's IP business model. Still, 20 years after they'd begun to build on that plan, many people — most, even — had no idea of what exactly it was, and is, that ARM does. Employees still had to explain how the company has never manufactured anything or even arranged for anything to be manufactured. Rather, in the words of its 2013 strategic report, it is "the world's leading semiconductor intellectual property (IP) supplier." Few people who heard increasing mentions of ARM's stellar stock market performance on BBC Radio 4 knew that it was essentially an R&D outsourcing company, which builds the technology that companies use to build things for themselves.

Those companies — the partners — who are all members of the ARM Connected Community that had been set up in 2003, numbered some 400 licensees by mid-2015, and between them they had licensed 1,200 designs. Having the partners tapping into a vast, complex and growing ecosystem is ARM's main strength.

In 2013, Tim Score (chief financial officer at the time) explained the ARM business model in plain terms to The Register: "If you phone us up and say, 'I'd love to buy a Cortex-A9. How much are they, please?' we can't quote you for a single device or even 10,000 devices. You'll have to go to someone like TI or Freescale or Samsung, who actually license and produce the chips. But we could quote you several tens of millions of dollars for a license to build one of your own." Or, to use VP of Technology Jem Davies' description of ARM's business model to his mother, ARM make knitting patterns for chips, and then make money every time someone makes a jumper from that pattern.

It's an ecosystem that enables partners to make deals between themselves — without ARM's intervention or involvement. An essential part of the model is that ARM doesn't even track what its partners do with its architecture. Some wouldn't tell ARM if it asked. Banking card manufacturers, for example, are naturally very secretive about what they do. They certainly don't tell their customers that they use ARM IP, and very often don't tell ARM what they do, either. Security is paramount, of course, and any clues as to a bank's IP could lead to the possible breaking into of that bank's accounts.

Academic Dr. James F. Moore was tasked by ARM with writing a 2012 assessment of its IP strategy. He reported that "multiple members of the ARM team" told him that the company deliberately and consciously "leaves room for others to differentiate on the chip." This "connecting the dots," as one ARM person put it, is critical to the company's business model. This broad base of partners and markets means that ARM is not overly reliant on any single company or consumer product for its future profits and cash.

It's a model that requires commitment and trust. ARM is part of partner companies' R&D teams, so there needs to be openness and honesty at the heart of the trading relationship, reinforced with trust, so that future plans are not jeopardized. Semiconductor companies may not get told as much by OEMs as ARM does, and ARM cannot — and does not — tell others about the depth and level of knowledge that has been revealed in the due course of doing its work.

ARM's own estimate is that it would cost each and every individual semiconductor company $100 million to do what ARM effectively does for them — a potential

25 × 25 Graham Budd

1 Who or what did you want to be when you grew up?   A linguist

2 What or who was your first obsession?   My ZX81

3 Who was your childhood hero (or is now)? $e^{15} + 1 = 0$

4 What's your secret?   Drink enough

5 *Star Trek* or *Star Wars*?   *Star Wars*

6 Did any book change your life? If so, what was it?   *The Gospel according to St Luke*

7 Favorite movie: *The Lord of the Rings* trilogy (2001-2003)

8 If you could hear only one piece of music again, what would it be?   *Mr Blue Sky* (1977), ELO

9 Vinyl, cassette, 8-track, CD, MP3, or streaming?   MP3

10 What do you prefer: Skype conference call or face-to-face meeting?   f2f meeting

11 Your favorite ARM product is: ARM7100

12 The best use of an ARM product is: In my hiking/cycling GPS

13 The best use of an ARM product would be ...   Housework robot

14 If you could bring anything back from extinction, what would it be?   The mammoth

15 Your favorite mode of transport is ...   Bicycle

16 What future invention would you like to make (or witness)?   Teleportation device

17 Ready, Aim, Fire, or Ready, Fire, Aim?   RAF

18 If you could ask one question of anybody, what would it be and to whom?   'What is the unifying theory of everything?'

19 When were you happiest?   With friends

20 What makes you angry?   Intolerance

21 What does love feel like?   Put others first

22 Bitcoin or dollars?   Dollars

23 How much is enough?   Sufficient

24 What is your greatest achievement?   Hasn't happened yet

25 Beach or adventure holiday?   Adventure

YEAR OF BIRTH   1968
COUNTRY OF BIRTH   UK
CITY OF RESIDENCE   Cambridge
UNIVERSITY + DEGREE   Cambridge: MA Engineering
TENURE AT ARM   1992-

Mali-400 MP4

DATE	October 2011
TECHNOLOGY	32 nm
TRANSISTORS	37M transistors, ~9.3M gates
SIZE	4.4 mm^2
POWER	2.1 mW/Mhz
FREQUENCY	266 MHz
ARCHITECTURE	Mali Utgard

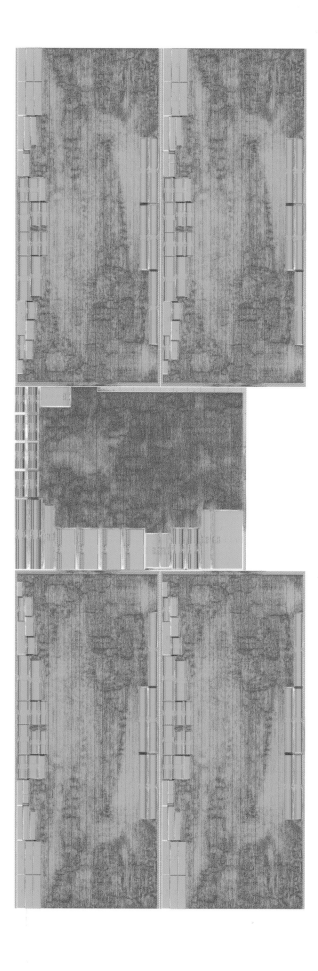

$20 billion cost burden that ARM saves the industry. As for ARM, those R&D costs are — ideally — recouped in revenues from licenses. The income from royalties is profit. In 2010, royalty revenues rose by 36 percent.

The same year, Calxeda raised the almost $50 million it needed to work toward its 2013 launch for a lower-powered server technology, an essential element of ARM's forward strategy. ARM also partnered with, among many others, Microsoft and started working with Linaro to develop Linux-based devices. The following year, Windows on ARM was unveiled at the Consumer Electronics Show 2011, and the first Windows on ARM devices shipped in 2012.

In 2011, ARM revenues were almost half a billion dollars and profits roughly a fifth of a billion dollars — despite it being, in the delicate phrase of the annual report, a "challenging year," with sovereign debt worries and semiconductor industry income slowing in each quarter. In March, Japan was hit by an infrastructure-damaging earthquake. Many factories had to halt or slow manufacture for months — which had a big effect on all sectors of the electronics industry. In October, Thailand suffered major flooding. Businesses were forced to close in more than 50 provinces. Many of them manufactured critical components for 45 percent of the world's hard disk drives.

Yet the number of ARM chips shipped rose to 7.9 billion, an increase of 30 percent on the previous year. Of those, 1.1 billion were microcontrollers, then ARM's fastest-growing market. The number of ARM-based processors in non-mobile devices grew by 50 percent. A record new 121 licenses were also signed that year, taking the total to nearly 850. Microsoft announced that the next version of Windows 8 would run on ARM processors, as would Office and Internet Explorer. Google announced that Chrome would work on ARM processors.

In the last quarter of 2011 the first Mali GPUs shipped, for use in smartphones and digital TVs. Two ARM processor-based servers were announced, by Applied Micro Circuits and HP, whose chips would be designed by Calxeda. Samsung's Galaxy Tab tablet, which used an ARM processor, came to market. "The mobile phone," said ARM's annual report, "is increasingly becoming a mobile computer and is likely to become one of the main ways that consumers connect to online products and services."

One of the strongest areas of growth in consumer electronics was in gaming, which had grown in popularity since the millennium to the point where it was greater than the music and movie industries' worldwide profits combined. In 2011, ARM announced its big.LITTLE processing system, saving up to 70 percent processor energy consumption in common workload tasks, yet still delivering console-quality gaming. A high performance processor works alongside a high efficiency processor, allowing either to take on tasks according to their respective capacities. (The big.LITTLE name is also something of a symbol of ARM's own culture and performance: the little company with a big place in its world.)

There was a strong start to 2012. A record 2 billion ARM-designed processors shipped in the first quarter, a substantial increase on forecasts. ARM's 9 percent rise in profits outperformed the rest of the semiconductor industry as a whole, which fell overall by 4 percent. By the second quarter, profits were up nearly a quarter, year on year. Over the year, revenues rose 16 percent, and profits by 41 percent. Average royalty rates also rose, mainly because chipmakers were starting to put multiple processor cores into devices. Three-quarters of the world's smartphones had a Cortex-A processor in the main chip.

By now there were more than a thousand companies in ARM's Connected

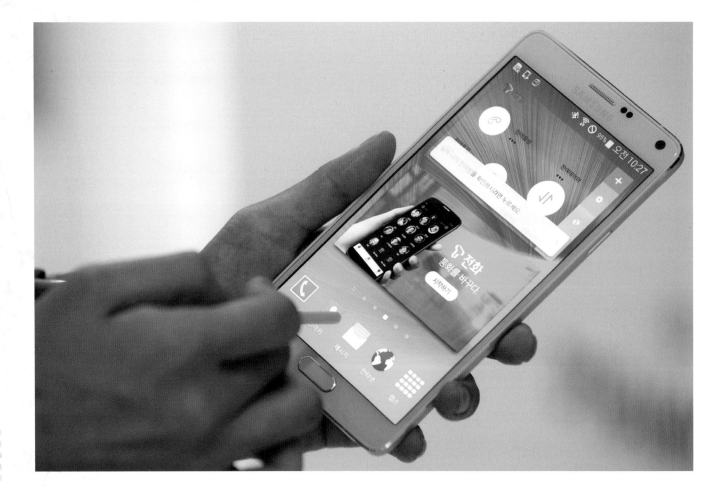

ABOVE The Samsung Galaxy Note 4 was one of the most successful Android smartphone launches of 2014 (4.5 million sold in the first month). It uses an ARM Mali-T760 GPU and a Cortex-A57 and Cortex -A53 big.LITTLE cluster.

Community. A quarter of license deals signed in 2012 were with companies taking out their first ARM license. And it was also the year that ARM introduced the 64-bit processor technology which would be the spearhead of a drive into the worlds of enterprise networking and servers. ARM's 2010 annual report had stated that, "Servers consume huge amounts of energy. Some of our partners are working on ARM technology-based chips which they believe can reduce energy by more than half." The first ARM 64-bit chips would ship in 2014.

In July 2012 Ian Drew, who had been EVP strategy since August 2011, became ARM's chief marketing officer and EVP business development. By night, though, he was someone else: Ian Drew, farmer, shepherd to 50 rare breed sheep, which he sells to friends and Michelin-starred restaurants. He has two Twitter handles, one for his ARM life, one for his sheep world. The second has far more followers. Far, far more.

A typical Drew day starts with 5:30 a.m. phone calls from his Wiltshire home and finishes, after half a dozen or more meetings, at 9 p.m. Then, in summer at least, he is out "mowing the fields on the tractor." He manages to do everything because (he says) he has ADHD and doesn't watch TV. Oh, and he only has three or four hours sleep.

In 2013 there were several significant changes to ARM's leadership. In January, Allen Wu was appointed president of ARM Greater China. Having worked in Silicon Valley, in both sales and engineering, he joined ARM in 2004. In September, Jennifer Duvalier joined ARM as executive vice president, people, after six years at the global events-led marketing and communications services business, UBM plc.

ARM Cortex-A57

DATE	June 5, 2013 LAC (IP for first tapeout)
TECHNOLOGY	TSMC 16FF+ (11-layer metal)
TRANSISTORS	6.9M gates (quad-core + 2M L2 excluding RAM (172M transistors incl. RAMs)
SIZE	8.9 mm^2 (quad-core + 2M shared L2)
FREQUENCY	2.1 GHz
POWER	750 mW Ptotal (307 mW/GHz Pdyn)
ARCHITECTURE	ARMv8-A
µARCHITECTURE	15-stage pipeline, out-of-order, 3-wide dispatch, 8-wide issue
DESCRIPTION	ARM's first high-end processor supporting 64-bit ARMv8 and AMBA 5 CHI architectures

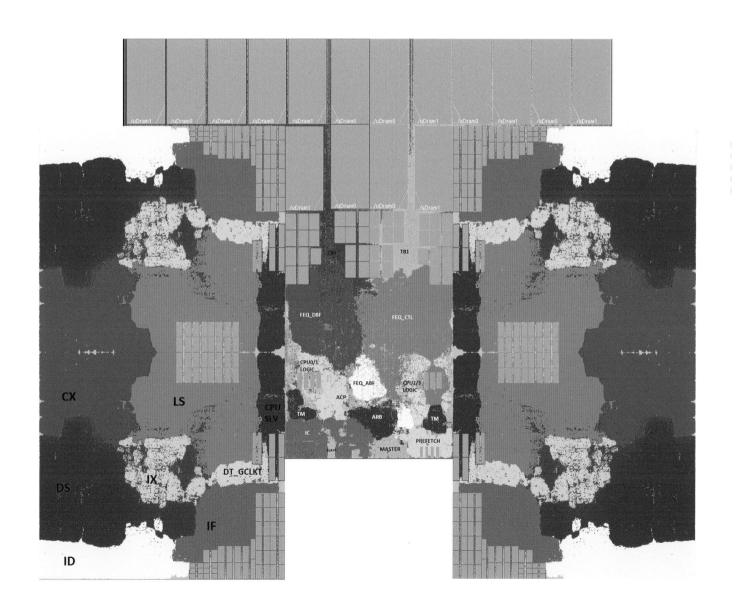

25x25 Dipesh I. Patel

YEAR OF BIRTH   1969
COUNTRY OF BIRTH   Uganda
CITY OF RESIDENCE   Saratoga, CA
UNIVERSITY + DEGREE
Loughborough University, UK,
BSc in Electronics and Electrical
Engineering. PhD also from same uni
TENURE AT ARM   1997-

1 **Who or what did you want to be when you grew up?**   Electronic Engineer

2 **What or who was your first obsession?**   Scalextric cars

3 **Who was your childhood hero (or is now)?**   Amitabh Bachchan

4 **What's your secret?**   Think in pictures and blocks and how it all connects together

5 *Star Trek* **or** *Star Wars*?   *Star Wars* when growing up because we didn't get *Star Trek* in Kenya

6 **Did any book change your life? If so, what was it?**   *Sophie's World* (1991), Jostein Gaarder — really made me think ... not sure it changed my life (yet!)

7 **Favorite movie:**   *Sholay* (1975)

8 **If you could hear only one piece of music again, what would it be?**   Ke Pag Ghunghroo Bandh (1982), Namak Halaal

9 **Vinyl, cassette, 8-track, CD, MP3, or streaming?**   MP3

10 **What do you prefer: Skype conference call or face-to-face meeting?**   Face-face meetings, though Skype is also good alternative

11 **Your favorite ARM product is:**   My phone

12 **The best use of an ARM product is:**   Video calls — allowing me to connect with my parents 1,000s of miles away

13 **The best use of an ARM product would be ...**   Holodeck

14 **If you could bring anything back from extinction, what would it be?**   T. Rex

15 **Your favorite mode of transport is ...**   Cars (would love to have one)

16 **What future invention would you like to make (or witness)?**   Teleportation — beam me up!

17 **Ready, Aim, Fire, or Ready, Fire, Aim?**   Ready, Aim, Fire

18 **If you could ask one question of anybody, what would it be and to whom?**   Mahatma Gandhi: 'How did you keep so calm and follow through with your beliefs?'

19 **When were you happiest?**   1986

20 **What makes you angry?**   When someone isn't listening

21 **What does love feel like?**   Every time I see my grandmother

22 **Bitcoin or dollars?**   Dollars

23 **How much is enough?**   Enough to stay happy

24 **What is your greatest achievement?**   Being able to support my parents and my family

25 **Beach or adventure holiday?**   Beach

ARM Acquisitions **1991-2015**

1 **Micrologic Solutions**
Cambridge, UK
1999

2 **Allant Software**
Walnut Creek, California, USA
2000

3 **EuroMIPS**
Sophia Antipolis, France
2000

4 **Infinite Designs**
Sheffield, UK
2000

5 **Noral Micrologics**
Blackburn, UK
2001

6 **Adelante Technologies**
Leuven, Belgium
2003

7 **Artisan Components**
Sunnyvale, California, USA
2004

8 **Axys Design Automation**
Irvine, California, USA
2004

9 **Keil Elektronik**
Munich, Germany
2005

10 **Falanx**
Trondheim, Norway
2006

11 **PowerEscape**
Olympia, Washington, USA
2006

12 **Soisic**
Grenoble, France
2006

13 **Logipard**
Lund, Sweden
2009

14 **Obsidian**
Austin, Texas, USA
2011

15 **Prolific**
Newark, California, USA
2011

16 **Geomerics**
Cambridge, UK
2013

17 **Sensinode**
Oulu, Finland
2013

18 **Duolog**
Dublin, Ireland
2014

19 **Offspark**
The Hauge, Netherlands
2015

20 **Sansa Security**
Kfar Netter, Israel
2015

21 **Wicentric**
San Diego, California, USA
2015

22 **Sunrise Micro Devices**
Deerfield Beach, Florida, USA
2015

On January 14, Khaled Benkrid, an Algiers-born former academic, joined ARM to run its worldwide university program. His first contact with the company had been as a lecturer at the University of Edinburgh. Conscious that his fellow teachers were using old technology, he approached ARM — the Austin, Texas, office, to be precise — looking for up-to-date boards for his students to use. Within a few days, his request received an okay from ARM, and within a week or two, they received a shipment of boards. Six months later, Khaled got an email from ARM, asking if he'd be interested in leaving his tenured academic post to become the company's worldwide university program manager. An hour-long phone call convinced him that ARM thinking was long-term, and in particular, that there was a strategic view of how to equip the next generation of engineers with the right skills for the modern economy. A few days later, he was met by a car at Stansted airport and taken to ARM's Cambridge headquarters. An outsider to the world of corporate tech business, the Cambridge atrium was something of a surprise to the academic. It has the look and feel of a startup, not a FTSE100 company, and as anyone who visits notices, at lunchtime ARM's CEO will leave his less than stately office and queue for his sandwich like everyone else.

ARM Profit per Employee **1991-2014**

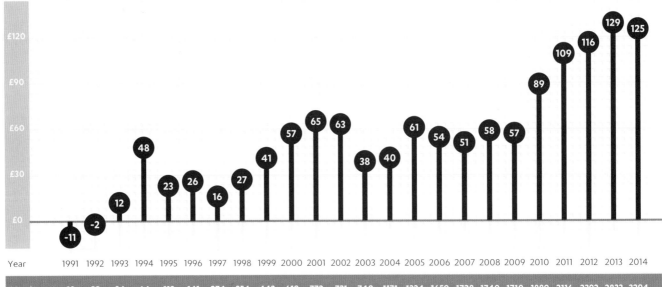

Year	1991	1992	1993	1994	1995	1996	1997	1998	1999	2000	2001	2002	2003	2004	2005	2006	2007	2008	2009	2010	2011	2012	2013	2014
Profit	-11	-2	12	48	23	26	16	27	41	57	65	63	38	40	61	54	51	58	57	89	109	116	129	125
Headcount	18	22	34	64	112	141	274	354	443	619	772	721	740	1171	1324	1659	1728	1740	1710	1889	2116	2392	2833	3294

Khaled's appointment was indicative of the company's increasing reach into the outside world. Although never likely to court publicity or desire a level of awareness among the public that many UK-based companies on the FTSE100 have, ARM knows that as the company grows it requires increasing injections of people with new ideas, but who can understand and want to be a part of the ARM plan. Educating future engineers in the ways of ARM is essential for the long-term future of the company. A successful company has to maintain its presence in the market while growing, adding new people and replacing those who retire.

In July 2013 Simon Segars (originally ARM's 16th employee) took over from Warren East — Warren claimed at the time that he was going to retire but has since become CEO of Rolls-Royce, which is a not inconsiderable challenge — to become the company's third CEO. A graduate of the universities of Sussex (B.Sc. in electronic engineering) and Manchester (M.Sc. in computer science), he had been at the company since 1990. An engineer, he led the development of the ARM7 and ARM9 in the early 1990s. These two CPUs were the power behind the first digital mobiles.

By 2013, three-quarters of the people in the world were using an electronic device based in ARM architecture — 50 billion chips in all. Worldwide, ARM-based technology was in 95 percent of smartphones, 80 percent of digital cameras and 35 percent of all electronic devices. Partners were shipping 2.5 billion chips a quarter: one for every three people. Over a year, that's about 1.5 per person—meaning that there are more chips in a year than there are people on the planet.

By 2013, though, only 4 percent of new licenses were for ARM7/9/11 chips. Growth — and the future — was in mobile computing: phones, tablets and their associated networks and infrastructure. That year, more than 1 billion smartphones shipped, which was a 50 percent increase on the previous year. It was the first year smartphones outsold feature phones.

25 × 25 Jenny Duvalier

1 Who or what did you want to be when you grew up?   An investigative journalist, initially sparked by Lois Lane and then by Nellie Bly, who circumnavigated the globe in 72 days in 1899, reporting for the New York World

2 What or who was your first obsession?   *Famous Five* books by Enid Blyton (1942-1963)

3 Who was your childhood hero (or is now)?   It's a tie between Katherine Hepburn and Eleanor Roosevelt: two strong women who broke the conventions of their time

4 What's your secret?   'It does not do to dwell on dreams and forget to live'. J. K. Rowling

5 *Star Trek* or *Star Wars*?   *Star Wars*: Princess Leia was a formative influence

6 Did any book change your life? If so, what was it?   Not one single book but many. *The Diving Bell and the Butterfly* (1997) by Jean-Dominique Bauby reminds me to treasure every moment and every human connection

7 Favorite movie: *Brief Encounter* (1945), for Celia Johnson's clipped vowels, Noel Coward's screenplay and Rachmaninoff's Piano Concerto no. 2

8 If you could hear only one piece of music again, what would it be?   *Fly Me to the Moon* by Julie London — it was playing in the delivery room as my daughter was born in 2000

9 Vinyl, cassette, 8-track, CD, MP3, or streaming?   Streaming

10 What do you prefer: Skype conference call or face-to-face meeting?   F2f

11 Your favorite ARM product is: Our connected, collaborative and high respect culture

12 The best use of an ARM product is: Mobile technologies that enable me to work flexibly, so that I can do my best work wherever I am

13 The best use of an ARM product would be ...   Reducing the impact of climate change through widespread use of low power technologies

14 If you could bring anything back from extinction, what would it be?   Privacy

15 Your favorite mode of transport is ...   My feet. Followed by a London black taxi

16 What future invention would you like to make (or witness)?   Teleportation — no more jet lag and carbon emissions from air travel

17 Ready, Aim, Fire, or Ready, Fire, Aim?   Ready, Aim, Fire

18 If you could ask one question of anybody, what would it be and to whom?   To the Empress Dowager Cixi, who controlled the Chinese government for 47 years until her death in 1908, and to her fellow modernising female monarch, Queen Victoria. My question to both would be whether they had any idea how profound and wide reaching the technology changes both introduced to their countries (industrialisation, railways ...) would be?

19 When were you happiest?   With my family, enjoying India

20 What makes you angry?   Social injustice

21 What does love feel like?   Like a great pair of shoes — always supportive, gorgeous and rarely painful

22 Bitcoin or dollars?   Dollars

23 How much is enough?   When there is enough to share with those in need

YEAR OF BIRTH   between Gen X and the millennial generation
COUNTRY OF BIRTH   England
CITY OF RESIDENCE   London
UNIVERSITY + DEGREE   University of Oxford, MA (Hons) English & French
TENURE AT ARM   2013-

24 What is your greatest achievement?   My family and my sanity

25 Beach or adventure holiday?   Adventure holiday

In August, ARM acquired Sensinode Oy, a Finnish company, which developed the low-power protocol stacks needed for wireless communication between sensors and hub. In May, Fitbit released the Fitbit Flex, a device worn on the wrist and which would, in time, link to smartphones. In July, the US consumer electronics corporation Best Buy started selling Pebble smartwatches that connected to the Internet via a smartphone. Stock sold out in five days. By the end of 2014 a million Pebbles had been sold.

Microcontroller sales also continued to rise. In 2009 ARM had 5 percent of the market; by 2013 it was 22 percent. Shipment of ARM's advanced Cortex-A family of processors doubled to 1.8 billion. As such chips command a higher royalty rate, ARM revenue in this area grew 19 percent, compared to an industry average of 1 percent.

The same year, ARMv8-A 64-bit architecture became available for server chip development, with the company expecting to have more than 20 percent of the server market by 2020. To that end, it partnered with IBM. The venerable computer company licensed processor designs — including Cortex-A15, Cortex-A12, Cortex-A7 and Cortex-M4 cores, plus the Mali-450 GPU — for its network equipment division. IBM's aim was to use the processors' mobile capabilities to enable it to build better networks for mobile phone operators.

In 2014 ARM technology was in 37 percent of smart electronic devices sold that year. In all, 12 billion ARM chips were shipped. As of 2014, the number of chips with ARM cores inside equated to roughly seven per person on the planet. By then there were 2 billion smartphones in the world, each one containing at least one ARM chip.

The first ARM 32-bit servers had come to market in 2012 and their 64-bit descendants arrived in 2014; 64-bit for mobiles from, notably, two Chinese fabless chipsters, Actions Semiconductor and Allwinner, made possible a $70 Android tablet. ARM estimated that in 2014 about 1.5 billion chips were sold into the "enterprise infrastructure" business: mobile phone base stations, Wi-Fi hotspots, corporate networks, TV distribution systems and, of course, the Internet. ARM's share of networking infrastructure chips doubled in 2014, from 5 to 10 percent.

25x25 Rene Haas

1 Who or what did you want to be when you grew up? A professional sportscaster, journalist, author — something information related.

2 What or who was your first obsession? Reading, absorbing information, and learning. I was reading all kinds of things by age 4.

3 Who was your childhood hero (or is now)? Not really sure I had one, but I was a big sports fan growing up. Now, I think heroes are people who give their lives for others. That defines heroism to me.

4 What's your secret? Umm ... it's a secret, so next question.

5 _Star Trek_ or _Star Wars_? _Star Trek_. But it's close.

6 Did any book change your life? If so, what was it? No one book changed my life. I am always learning and reading. Every day I learn something that changes me a little.

7 Favorite movie: _The Godfather_ — it's about family, power, history and full of great quotes ("Drop the gun ... keep the cannoli.")

8 If you could hear only one piece of music again, what would it be? Rolling Stones: Gimme Shelter. No specific meaning, just like the music.

9 Vinyl, cassette, 8-track, CD, MP3, or streaming? Streaming and the next format, which will be even better. To me, each format is better than the one that precedes it.

10 What do you prefer: Skype conference call or face-to-face meeting? I don't even have a Skype ID ...

11 Your favorite ARM product is: IPad (I am assuming that the answer we are looking for is not Cortex-M0 ...)

12 The best use of an ARM product is: Reading, learning and getting smarter.

13 The best use of an ARM product would be ... See above.

14 If you could bring anything back from extinction, what would it be? I don't think I would, it's not meant to be. But I am curious how we put a man on the moon in 1969, kept continuous radio communication, brought them back safely, yet my mobile phone still drops coverage in 2015. I'd like to talk to those guys at NASA who made it all work (I assume they are not extinct!)

15 Your favorite mode of transport is ... When someone else is driving except me.

16 What future invention would you like to make (or witness)? Time travel. Could change everything (literally!).

17 Ready, Aim, Fire, or Ready, Fire, Aim? Ready fire aim.

18 If you could ask one question of anybody, what would it be and to whom? Anyone who can give a definitive answer to 'what happens when you die?'

19 When were you happiest? My kids being born.

20 What makes you angry? Any type of politics, inefficiency, lack of directness.

21 What does love feel like? Pretty much the best feeling there is.

22 Bitcoin or dollars? RMB.

23 How much is enough? On the material side — I think most people can get away with far less. People matter more than material things.

24 What is your greatest achievement? Two teenage daughters, that so far are better adjusted and better prepared for life than I was at their age.

25 Beach or adventure holiday? Adventure.

YEAR OF BIRTH 1962
COUNTRY OF BIRTH USA
CITY OF RESIDENCE Shanghai, China
UNIVERSITY + DEGREE Clarkson University, Bachelors of Science, Electrical and Computer Engineering
TENURE AT ARM 2013-

Many of these chips went into 4G base stations, and represented perfectly what had become the most significant development between 2010 and 2015 for ARM: the extension to 64-bit and ARMv8 architecture. They had opened up the server market to ARM, where the profit margins are very high. And, as the ARM ecosystem is open to many players, 64-bit architecture opened it to the server market.

Simultaneously ARM's Mali graphics processor began to gain market share. The Mali was developed in Trondheim from work originally done by graphics pioneers Falanx Microsystems, a company founded in 2000, which was bought by ARM in 2006. The strategy was emblematic. When ARM makes acquisitions across the world, whatever the newly bought companies were previously, they become the nucleus for new ARM design centers. At one point, ARM made an offer to buy a fabless chip company who were in field-programmable gate array technology. The plan had been to license the technology as IP and keep the fabless chip business to kickstart the configurable microcontroller market, but ARM were outbid by Xilinx at the last minute. In fact the failure to buy the fabless company proved to be a good thing. Had they bought it, ARM would have been competing with their own customers. It could have been the downfall of the company.

The model certainly worked with Falanx Microsystems, though. In 2014, 550 million Mali chips shipped. There was a Mali in more than 75 percent of Chinese-manufactured application processors. To many people, the ARM business model is the company's biggest asset, because expansion is only limited by imagination. The ARM ecosystem is unparalleled, with everyone doing their bit, in collaboration. It's a small company but its ecosystem scales it up, creating more for — and from — less, making a better product for the customer. It's a powerful and extendable business model that could, perhaps, work in other markets. Not that there's any desire to try that.

The original founders who decided they would not fabricate made, without knowing it, a visionary decision in 1990. It's the original DNA of the company, to which manufacturers add their own ingredients. That original decision to put collaboration and working with others at the center of everything, to open up to as large a number of partners as possible, means that there is no limit to the number of partners that ARM can work with. Problems that might arise in the industry are faced collaboratively, and fixed together (pretty much, anyway). Similarly, changes in the desires of the consumer market are addressed in time to cover all outcomes.

Quite obviously the biggest changes and developments between 2010 and 2015 came in mobile technology, and whereas in 2010 only 3 billion of the 22 billion-unit chip market went into mobile phones, since then smartphones have become ubiquitous. And now there are even Wi-Fi-connected Barbie dolls.

As always, Moore's Law holds. Whereas previously supercomputers had been the norm, ARM are building a lot of functionality into smaller chips, making them more efficient and more miniaturized. There are now chips the thickness of a human hair — less than a square millimeter, barely visible — which are powerful, much more powerful than the processor used for the Apollo moon landing.

In February 2015, ARM announced its most powerful design to date, the 64-bit Cortex-A72 processor core. This would put more muscle and drive in the next generation of smartphones and tablets, particularly when handling gaming. Though it had twice the performance of its predecessor, the Cortex-A57, the A72 used only about half the power. It was expected that, by 2016, high-end handhelds would have four A72s and four Cortex-A53s — that's eight ARMs in your hand.

Cortex-A53 Quad-Core

DATE	August 2013 LAC release
TECHNOLOGY	28 nm
TRANSISTORS	6M gates excluding RAMs
SIZE	6.3 mm^2 for an MP4 configuration with 32K L1 caches, 1MB L2 cache
FREQUENCY	1 GHz
POWER	100 mW/Ghz (0.1 mW/MHz in old money)
ARCHITECTURE	ARMv8-A
µARCHITECTURE	8 stage in-order with symmetric dual-issue
DESCRIPTION	The first ARMv8 LITTLE processor

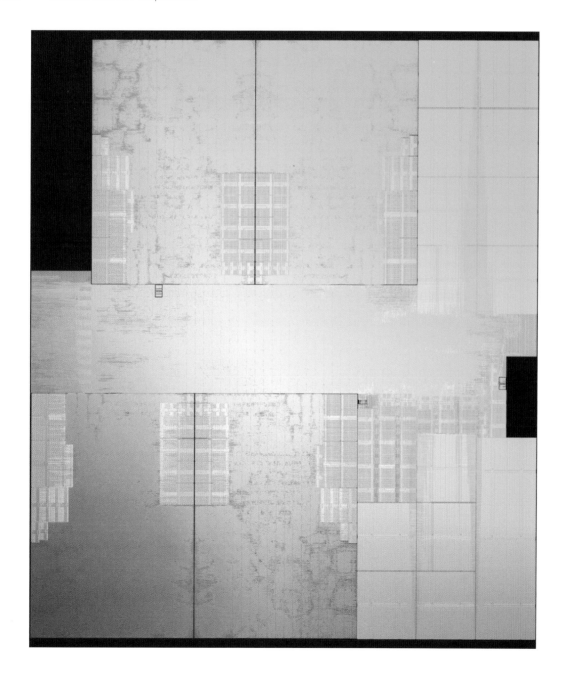

ARM Chips **3rd Parties**

StrongARM (Digital)

 SA-110:
- 5-stage pipeline
- 16 KB / 16 KB, MMU
- 100-206 MHz

 SA-1100:
- 5-stage pipeline
- 16 KB / 8 KB, MMU
- 100-206 MHz

Faraday (Faraday Technology)

 FA510:
- 6-stage pipeline
- Up to 32 KB / 32 KB cache, MPU
- 1.26 DMIPS/MHz 100–200 MHz

 FA526:
- 6-stage pipeline
- Up to 32 KB / 32 KB cache, MMU
- 1.26 MIPS/MHz 166-300 MHz

 FA626:
- 8-stage pipeline
- 32 KB / 32 KB cache, MMU
- 1.35 DMIPS/MHz 500 MHz

 FA606TE:
- 5-stage pipeline
- No cache, no MMU
- 1.22 DMIPS/MHz 200 MHz

 FA626TE:
- 8-stage pipeline
- 32 KB / 32 KB cache, MMU
- 1.43 MIPS/MHz 800 MHz

FMP626TE:
- 8-stage pipeline, SMP
- 32 KB / 32 KB cache, MMU
- 1.43 MIPS/MHz 500 MHz

FA726TE:
- 13-stage pipeline, dual issue
- 32 KB / 32 KB cache, MMU
- 2.4 DMIPS/MHz 1000 MHz

XScale (Intel/Marvell)

 XScale:
- 7-stage pipeline, Thumb, Enhanced DSP instructions
- 32 KB / 32 KB, MMU
- 133–400 MHz

 Bulverde:
- Wireless MMX, Wireless Speed Step added
- 32 KB / 32 KB, MMU
- 312–624 MHz

 Monahans:
- Wireless MMX2 added
- 32 KB / 32 KB (L1), optional L2 cache up to 512 KB, MMU
- Up to 1.25 GHz

Sheeva (Marvell)

 Feroceon:
- 5-8 stage pipeline, single-issue
- 16 KB / 16 KB, MMU
- 600–2000 MHz

 Jolteon:
- 5-8 stage pipeline, dual-issue
- 32 KB / 32 KB, MMU
- 600–2000 MHz

PJ1 (Mohawk):
- 5-8 stage pipeline, single-issue, Wireless MMX2
- 32 KB / 32 KB, MMU
- 1.46 DMIPS/MHz 1.06 GHz

 PJ4:
- 6-9 stage pipeline, dual-issue, Wireless MMX2, SMP
- 32 KB / 32 KB, MMU
- 2.41 DMIPS/MHz 1.6 GHz

Snapdragon (Qualcomm)

 Scorpion:
- 1 or 2 cores. ARM / Thumb / Thumb-2 / DSP / SIMD / VFPv3 FPU / NEON (128-bit wide)
- 256 KB L2 per core
- 2.1 DMIPS/MHz per core

 Krait:
- 1, 2, or 4 cores. ARM / Thumb / Thumb-2 / DSP / SIMD / VFPv4 FPU / NEON (128-bit wide)
- 4 KB / 4 KB L0, 16 KB / 16 KB L1, 512 KB L2 per core
- 3.3 DMIPS/MHz per core

Ax (Apple)

 Swift:
- 2 cores. ARM / Thumb / Thumb-2 / DSP / SIMD / VFPv4 FPU / NEON
- L1: 32 KB / 32 KB, L2: 1 MB
- 3.5 DMIPS/MHz per core

 Cyclone:
- 2 cores. ARM / Thumb / Thumb-2 / DSP / SIMD / VFPv4 FPU / NEON / TrustZone / AArch64
- L1: 64 KB / 64 KB, L2: 1 MB, L3: 4 MB
- 1.3 - 1.4 GHz

 Cyclone Gen. 2:
- 2 or 3 cores. ARM / Thumb / Thumb-2 / DSP / SIMD / VFPv4 FPU / NEON / TrustZone / AArch64
- L1: 64 KB / 64 KB, L2: 1 or 2 MB, L3: 4 MB
- 1.4 - 1.5 GHz

X-Gene (Applied Micro)

 X-Gene:
- 64-bit, quad issue, SMP, 64 cores
- Cache, MMU, virtualization
- 3 GHz (4.2 DMIPS/MHz per core)

Denver (Nvidia)

 Denver:
- 2 cores. AArch64, 7-wide superscalar, in-order, dynamic code optimization, 128 MB optimization cache
- 128 KB I / 64 KB D
- Up to 2.5 GHz

ThunderX (Cavium)

 ThunderX:
- 64-bit, with two models with 8-16 or 24-48 cores (×2 w/two chips)
-
- Up to 2.5 GHz

K12 (AMD)

 K12:
-
-
-

The prospect was described by The Register as "the equivalent of shoving data center tech into your pocket."

As ARM's success continues, the company has had to contend with the attention of investors and shareholders, among them numerous institutions — just 1 percent of shares are held by people in the company. As of mid-2015, ARM was telling investors that the company had a long-term growth story, that it will grow royalties as chips get used in more products, enabling more ARM technology to be used.

By the time that its 25th anniversary was coming round, ARM had become a worldwide company, albeit one with a strong British base. Though headquartered in Cambridge, its UK employees accounted for just 41 percent of the worldwide workforce, which was housed in 30 offices across 14 countries. By the start of 2015, headcount had risen by 50 percent from 2010, to around 4,000, across 35 offices in 18 countries.

ARM licenses were even less UK-centered — just 1 percent of the total compared to 15 percent in Europe, 39 percent in the Asia/Pacific region and 45 percent in North America. In 1998 by comparison, those figures had been 53 percent US, 31 percent Asia/Pacific and 16 percent Europe.

That there are no customers for ARM in Cambridge is good for the company. In the early days the team spent a lot of time in Japan and the US; culturally, the UK is somewhere between the two. Something of the Japanese idea of consensus has rubbed off on ARM — even though, at times, it has created a problem. Who takes a decision? When Mike Inglis (an ARM executive from 2002 to 2013, who left to sail his boat round the world) had not been at the company that long, he asked, in a meeting, "When are we going to make a decision?" He was told it had already been taken, half an hour or so earlier. He just hadn't noticed. That's the way decisions were made at ARM.

Many at the company suggest that other people think ARM is much bigger than it is, but at the same time, it still feels small. In the early days, the company motto, of sorts, was "Hard work but fun." It might be more organized now but there is still a healthy amount of anarchy around the place. ARM is still disrespectful of formality. ▪

Chapter 7
... and Beyond

As you started reading this sentence, there were, roughly, 7 billion people in the world. Now there are another 17 or so. Population increases by 2.37 people every second. By the time you reach the end of this chapter, there will be something like an extra 25,000 or so people you'll be sharing our planet with.

In 2014, 65 billion chips were shipped worldwide, although only 33 billion of those contained processors, of which 12 billion were ARM architecture — a 16 percent increase on 2013. That is, 37 percent of the world's processor chips that shipped in 2014 used ARM architecture, up from previous year's 35 percent. At the same rate of increase that figure would be 14 billion in 2015.

There are some 125 ARM-powered products shipped every second, many of them with more than one ARM chip, so that's even more chips. In the first quarter of 2015, 3.8 billion ARM chips shipped, more than 450 a second. As of mid-2015, ARM-based chips were entering the world at something like two hundred times the rate of people. Since you started reading this chapter, more than a thousand ARM chips have gone to work somewhere.

By 2015 ARM was a truly global company. Head to London Heathrow Terminal 3 on any given Monday and chances are you'll find at least one ARM executive or engineer waiting for his or her long-haul flight. (Most likely it will be "his" plane rather than "hers." Around 80 percent of ARM engineers are men, compared to an industry average of 90 percent.)

Low-cost smartphones are now prevalent — many cost less than $100, even without subsidies. Some cost as little as $35. This has been made possible by ARM's low power, high performance technology and partnership business model. The Chinese Gionee P2S phone, for example, had at its core both an ARM Cortex-A7 CPU and an ARM Mali-400 GPU.

A 2015 report by IHS Technology said that 72.4 million smartphones had been sold in China the previous year, up from just 4.6 million in 2013. The report predicted sales would double again 2015, to 144.1 million, then 219.8 million in 2016 and 298.5 million in 2017. In February 2015 the online investment site Motley Fool, in a piece titled "Is ARM Holdings the best company in the FTSE100?," commented, "ARM is in the perfect

142

ABOVE   ARM CEO Warren East says farewell to the company in the Cambridge Atrium, summer 2013, with Simon Segars waiting his turn.

position to benefit from this kind of growth." It wasn't alone in thinking that, either.

Mobile phones and apps are transforming the developing world. Where only one in three have access to the Internet and few have bank accounts, money can be transferred, securely, from phone to phone. In sub-Saharan Africa, farmers can use their mobile to keep track of crop and livestock prices at market. Phones are also used to provide education — via both voice and written material — thus lowering the barrier to knowledge. Businesses have learned how to improve productivity, parents have learned to prevent and treat childhood diseases.

As of 2015, more than 1.1 billion people were using smartphones and tablets. ARM predicts that, over the next few years, up to 1 billion more people will get their first mobile phone or tablet and become "connected." A further 2 to 3 billion people will join the connected and global economy by 2025, by which time nearly 80 percent of all Internet connections could be through mobile devices. Further, of all technologies, it's the mobile phone to which people have the strongest attachment. A 2014 study found people happier to leave home without their wallet than their smartphone. It's likely that the words "mobile phone" and "smartphone" will leave the language. A phone, by definition, will be smart and mobile — as smart and mobile as the person using it. Maybe even the word "phone" will go the way of, say, "wireless." In a speech at Computex in June 2015, Ian Drew didn't mention the word "phone" once. Innovation happens in bursts, not straight lines, and while the Internet has been the burst over the first ten years of the century, it has led us to the point where nearly everyone wants to be connected. Half the people in the Western world, when they wake up, check Facebook or their email before they do anything else — usually even before they get out of bed.

The opportunity for ARM in the connected world is vast. Devices need to be able to work all day and so require low power consumption. Both the Internet connection and the phone need to be fast enough; phones need to be rich, both in terms of graphics and content. ARM have played a significant part in making that possible. The company has provided key building blocks for the interconnectivity of mobile devices globally.

In that February posting, Motley Fool went on to write of ARM, "The group is innovative, cash-generative, a leader in its field, produces a high return on equity and is currently sitting on a huge pile of cash — five of the most attractive traits any business can have." The piece then looked into the future and added, "as the company now dominates the smartphone microchip market, ARM is now looking to dominate the Internet of Things market."

The phrase "Internet of Things" (IoT) is now in its second decade. It was coined in 1999, by Kevin Ashton, an English entrepreneur and co-founder of MIT's Auto-ID Labs.

BELOW ARM's focus moves eastwards.

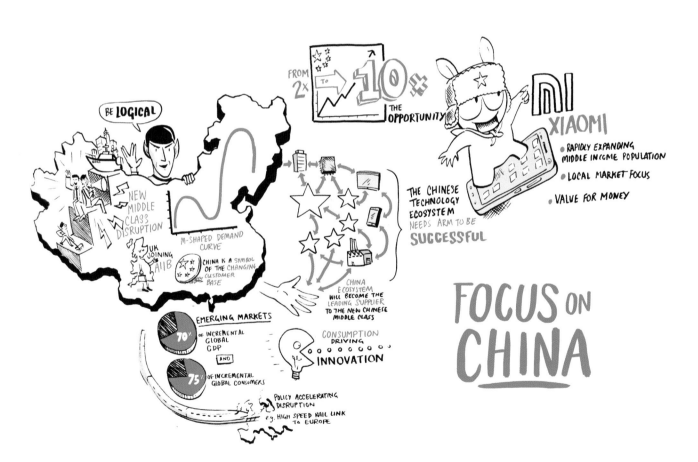

ABOVE   The ARM APM has grown from being a table full in a barn, to filling the grounds of a Cambridge college.

He began to form the idea in Birmingham, where he was working at Procter & Gamble. He realized he could significantly improve the company's supply chain management by using radio-frequency identification chips to store and transfer information, securely. The same year, ARM's annual report dreamed of the future: "Imagine ... ordering your groceries will have been done by your refrigerator, which will contact the store directly and arrange automatic delivery. Hooking up the domestic appliances in your home to the Internet so that you can communicate with them, and they with you, will certainly be with us in the not too distant future, and ARM will be an enabler of these developments."

The Internet of Things began to gain purchase, if at first only as an idea. In 2001, in an MIT Auto-ID White Paper, D. L. Brock described a vision of a "Smart World." That is, "an intelligent infrastructure linking objects, information and people through the computer network." He looked forward to creating "open standards, protocols and languages to facilitate worldwide adoption of this network." That is the basis for an Internet of Things.

Yet, the development of the Internet of Things has been slower — far slower perhaps — than predicted. In the 2010 ARM annual report, CEO Warren East wrote about washing machines with enough intelligence to decide how much detergent to use based on how dirty the clothes are, and spin the drum using more energy-efficient control algorithms. Such technology, though, has taken time to reach the consumer market. The ARM 2012 report gave a description of what would be needed for the IoT

Chips per Segment **1991-2014**

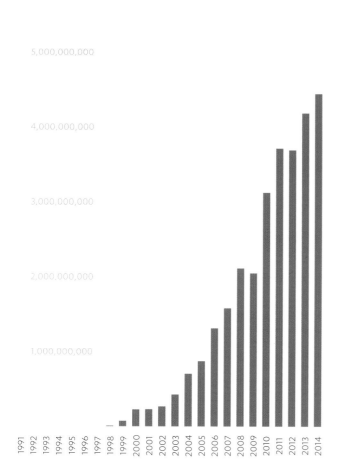

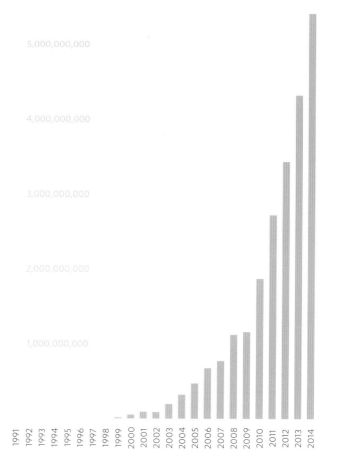

Mobile:
35,550,112,482
Total chips between 1991-2014

Non-Mobile:
27,910,760,924
Total chips between 1991-2014

ARM**25** × 25-year-olds

We asked ARM colleagues born in 1990 to answer 25 questions about life, art, work and the future. Where the question required an either/or answer we've calculated the percentage responses. But we've also picked the most "interesting" answers to the rest of the questions and given the individual's name after.

1 **Who or what did you want to be when you grew up?**
A cement truck
Oivind Boge (graduate engineer, MPG), Trondheim

2 **What or who was your first obsession?**
Where did I come from?
Lu Zhang (graduate design engineer, CPU), Austin

3 **Marvel or DC?**
Marvel 52 percent, DC 36, neither 12

4 **What does ARM mean to you?**
First job
Neetha Lenka (technical author, PEG), Cambridge

5 **How old is "old"?**
46 (average of ages given in response)

6 **Did any book change your life? If so, what was it?**
So many! Matilda (1988, Roald Dahl) for showing that it was OK to be as into books as I was, growing up, and Harry Potter (1997-2007, J. K. Rowling) for bringing together people of my generation for years after. The Narnia books (1950-56, C. S. Lewis) for getting me into fantasy in the first place … This is really hard!
Kathy Hadfield (graduate technical author, PEG), Cambridge

7 **Playstation or Xbox?**
Playstation 34 percent, Xbox 38, neither 28

8 **If you could hear only one piece of music again, what would it be?**
Cosmic background radiation ambient sound
Akash B. S. (design engineer, PDG), Noida

9 **Facebook, Instagram or SnapChat?**
Facebook 66 percent, Instagram 16, Snapchat 2, WhatsApp 8, none 8

10 **What's the worst job you've ever had?**
Coating sponges in heated beef gelatine and then weighing them. I smelled like wet dog for weeks
John Burke (graduate engineer, SSG), Galway

11 **The most exciting thing you've done in the past 25 years is …**
Getting school exams cancelled by spreading the news there was a bomb in the building
Anon (design engineer, PDG)

12 **The best use of an ARM product is:**
The Rubik's Cube solver
Thomas Tarridec (graduate engineer, CPU), Sophia Antipolis

13 **The best use of an ARM product would be:**
Traveling through time
Yoann Fanthou (graduate engineer, CPU), Sophia Antipolis

14 **If you could bring anything back from extinction, what would it be?**
BJT (Bipolar Junction Transistor)
Shreelekha Singh (designer engineer, PDG), Noida

15 **Your favorite mode of transport is …**
Walking 24 percent, cycling 20, driving 12, airplane 12, train 8, submarine 4, skiing 4, quadbike 4, quadski 4, grandfather's shoulders 4, jetpack 4

16 **What future invention would you like to make (or witness)?**
Mind control
Xuan Gu (graduate engineer, SSG), Sheffield

17 **Ready, Aim, Fire, or Ready, Fire, Aim?**
Ready, Aim, Fire 72 percent; R, F, A 8 [A, F 8 percent; A, R, F 4; F 4; neither 4 percent]

18 **If you could ask one question of anybody, what would it be, and to whom?**
To the future me: What would he (I) have done differently?
Viktor Szentgyorgyi (engineer, SSG), Budapest

19 **When were you happiest?**
When I was a kid, without a care in the world
Neha Amlani (internal communications coordinator, ADHR), Cambridge

20 **What makes you angry?**
The Nyquist stability criterion
Fredrik Brosser (graduate engineer,
PEG), Cambridge

21 **What does love feel like?**
Like a piece of code you've written that
works the first time you try it
Francois Donati (engineer, CPU),
Sophia Antipolis

22 **Bitcoin or dollars?**
Bitcoin 16 percent, dollars 64, neither 20

23 **How much is enough?**
This much — I'm tired of answering
questions ...
Akash B. S. (design engineer, PDG),
Noida

24 **Would you rather have a**
hovering skateboard or a personal
jetpack?
Hovering skateboard 38 percent,
jetpack 58, neither 4

25 **What's your secret?**
874f51066cbaccb73f0ea12526dc99a3f46a
437495ec8995dde1cda51269056b16 bf75f
8419db029f3b6ed8e364c7df39ff442dc01
d12f1b7fa5fdfa1b5b7642
Pedro Palhares de Campos (Python
web developer, DSG), Cambridge

[Most common answers: "Not telling,"
36 percent; "If I told you, it wouldn't be a
secret," 20]

ABOVE   "Me! Me! Me! I was born in 1990, Miss ..."

ABOVE   Tony Fadell, former VP of the iPod division at Apple (2006), continued to harness ARM technology when creating the Nest Labs range of Internet of Things consumer products such as this smoke alarm and thermostat.

to work. There were three elements: 1. Low-cost smart devices that combine one or more environmental (i.e. temperature, pressure) sensors. 2. A computer to process sensor data. 3. A wireless connection to the Internet. The sensor reports back to its "home base," which does the math, then wirelessly contacts the relevant piece of equipment in which a microcontroller oversees the delivery of, say, the water or the drug. In 2012 an ARM executive publicly suggested it would take about three years before vendors would start to see real takeup of mbed-powered IoT devices. It seems that 2015 is the year the IoT really started to get there.

In 2010 ARM priced a cheap-but-smart microcontroller at less than a dollar. By 2012 an ARM Cortex-M0 was yours for 49 cents. "Intelligence starting at $0.50" was the phrase. That year ARM Cortex-M-based devices were shipped at an annual compound growth rate of 40 percent. They were getting even cheaper, too. By 2016, it was predicted, an ARM Cortex-M0 would cost less than 30 cents. Other basic but central hardware was heading the same direction. Wi-Fi, Bluetooth, sensors, camera and GPS chips would all be up to 50 percent cheaper by 2016.

The Internet of Things is truly on its way. While the mobile Internet system is 10 billion units strong, the Internet of Things is 10 times that size. There were just two varieties of domestic computers: desktop and laptop. Mobile computing came in a wider range of forms, from smartphone to tablet to phablet. The IoT, though, will

have millions of different forms, devices and apps. Nor will it be a one-size-fits-all technology. An air-conditioning sensor has quite different requirements to an electric motor controller. Both will, though, ARM thinks, be run by its technology.

The future looks different, of course, the closer you get to it, but only sci-fi writers of the 20th century could have envisioned something like 2015's 1 mm^3 complete self-powered chip — actually a stack of four chips on a battery with a solar cell on top — which can be powered by room light and, if coated in plastic, could be surgically implanted into a living creature. Sci-fi moviemakers might show something that looks like a piece of clingfilm and which turns out to be electronics printed on to plastic, and which could be wrapped around a can of Coke. Yet both are very real.

By 2015, domestic lighting and gas boilers were already commonly controlled via smartphones. An IoT device could be small enough to fit in the dimple of a golf ball, cost less than 50 cents and have a battery life of months. A little more than $100 buys a smartphone-controlled paper airplane, with an ARM-based chip at the controls. Ovens can be controlled from smartwatches. Among other technologies transformed will be electric car charging, building automation, domestic utility management, smoke alarms, security cameras, toys and health monitors.

The Internet of Things offers a multitude of potentialities. Beyond the home, IoT devices can be used to manage irrigation systems to increase crop yields with less water;

ABOVE A Cortex-M0 stand-alone energy harvesting 1 mm^3 IoT system with solar cell and battery, developed by Michigan University, next to a CR3032 battery.

to run remote medical monitoring systems which liberate patients from the confines of the hospital; to help develop "smarter" cities, via transport systems which can support larger populations with less congestion; or to enable factories to break away from the shackles of mass manufacture and make a far wider range and variety of products.

For some people at ARM the most exciting part of IoT is infrastructure, for example sensors that can be put into parking spaces then linked together wirelessly and attached to a database, through which you can pay using an app. It also enables variable pricing, giving a driver the choice of paying a premium to park close to their destination or paying less and walking from a less congested and therefore cheaper area.

ARM partners work across the whole range of the IoT. Onfarm offers "precision agriculture," ensuring the right amount of water, seed and fertilizer is delivered to the right part of the right field at the optimum moment in the optimum quantity. EnLight produces streetlights that respond smartly, quickly and more efficiently to changes in the environment. Syrinix specializes in detection of pipeline leaks, preventing potentially catastrophic failures. Scandau's Scout improves the management of chronic disease, wirelessly, at a distance. ARM is working with IBM on its Smart Cities program. Via Wi-Fi or Bluetooth, street lights will sense how many people are nearby and adjust their light levels accordingly — a more fine-grained system than one using motion detectors.

The Taiwanese company M2Communication only opened for business in 2012, but by 2015 its electronic shelf label system was already the market leader. It's a communication network system that enables shops to update prices remotely on a 6,000-strong product line — while the products are still on the shelf. By the end of 2015 some 250,000 products will have been labeled with this technology. Its access point, router and labels are all powered by an ARM Cortex-M0 based microcontroller from the Taiwan-based specialist Nuvoton.

BELOW In 1949 this Vision of the Future had people dreaming of the connected house. Almost eighty years later, the Internet of Things is making that dream come true…

In the developing world, low-cost peripherals can be linked to phones to help manage healthcare in remote regions. In sport, location and spin sensors are being added to footballs and basketballs, enabling footballers to find just the right way to bend the ball and basketball players to work out just how to pop a shot at the optimum angle. These new possibilities are also enthusing a new generation to create and innovate, by lowering the cost barrier. One entrepreneur used the technology to build a prototype for less than $100.

It is predicted that by 2020 there will be 26 billion IoT units installed around the world, including 1 million smart parking spaces and as many as 1 billion smart utility meters in homes. According to a 2013 OECD report, Building Blocks for Smart Networks, the average family of four (two parents, two teenagers) will have 50 Internet-connected devices in their house, compared with about 10 in 2012. Juniper Research predicted that, in 2017, 70 million smart wearables will ship — watches and glasses, baby monitors and posture monitors, health monitors and fitness clips. Smart jewelry, even.

To face this IoT future, ARM prepared itself in various ways. In 2015, for example, it bought Offspark, a Dutch firm specializing in security software. It then gave software free to smart device manufacturers, to make sure it had established, before its competitors, a beachhead in the IoT market.

In 2009 ARM set up the mbed community, which was 33 partners strong, with 70,000 programmers signed up to its site by mid-2015. In October 2014 ARM announced mbedOS, which allows various different — and competing — companies to work together smoothly so that applications can talk to sensors and microcontrollers. No matter whether the chips are from Atmel, Marvell, ST, Freescale or NXP. mbedOS enables high-level software to manage and get information from many other small, simple devices. A lot has changed since the stand-alone systems of the BBC Micro, and we now need to create secure systems connecting many devices together. As Mike Muller told The Register, "It's no longer the 1980s where you had to use assembly language. You can do it more efficiently now, and development time really matters." The mbedOS is designed for the Cortex-M family, ARM's 32-bit microcontroller cores — they sleep till woken up by an external event, then deal with it, deciding whether or not they need to send a signal higher up the line. They then go back to sleep, saving on power. Faster, cheaper, better.

As part of ARM's preparation for the future, in January 2014 Simon Segars led a restructuring of the company, combining all its divisions into one product development team, led by the president of product groups, Pete Hutton. Since joining ARM in 2008 Pete had taken responsibility for the development and delivery of all product groups, including processors, Mali media processors including GPUs, and Artisan Physical IP.

The same month, ARM's chairman Sir John Buchanan stepped down for health reasons. Stuart Chambers, former Pilkington plc chief executive and group chief executive of Nippon Sheet Glass, joined the board and took over as chairman in March. That spring, two non-executive directors, Philip Rowley and Eric Meurice, left the board, while Dr. John Liu, a Chinese national, joined in December. Antonio J. Viana, who had been at ARM since 1999, became EVP and president of commercial and global development — he had previously overseen development systems sales in North America and run the ARM foundry program worldwide. ARM also hired new people: chief information officer Andy Smith came from spending five years with "one of the

Chips per Geographic Location **1991-2014**

Geographic Locations

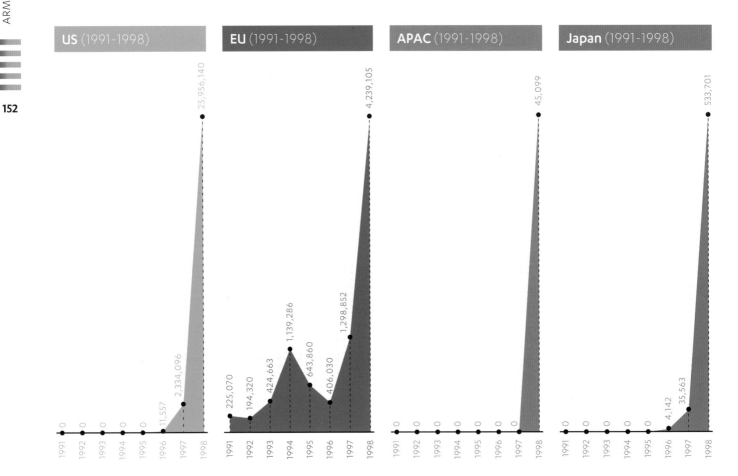

| US (1991-1998) | EU (1991-1998) | APAC (1991-1998) | Japan (1991-1998) |

US: 1991 0, 1992 0, 1993 0, 1994 0, 1995 0, 1996 11,557, 1997 2,334,096, 1998 25,956,140

EU: 1991 225,070, 1992 194,320, 1993 424,663, 1994 1,139,286, 1995 643,860, 1996 406,030, 1997 1,298,852, 1998 4,239,105

APAC: 1991 0, 1992 0, 1993 0, 1994 0, 1995 0, 1996 0, 1997 0, 1998 45,099

Japan: 1991 0, 1992 0, 1993 0, 1994 0, 1995 0, 1996 4,142, 1997 35,563, 1998 533,701

All Geographic Locations (1999 - 2014)

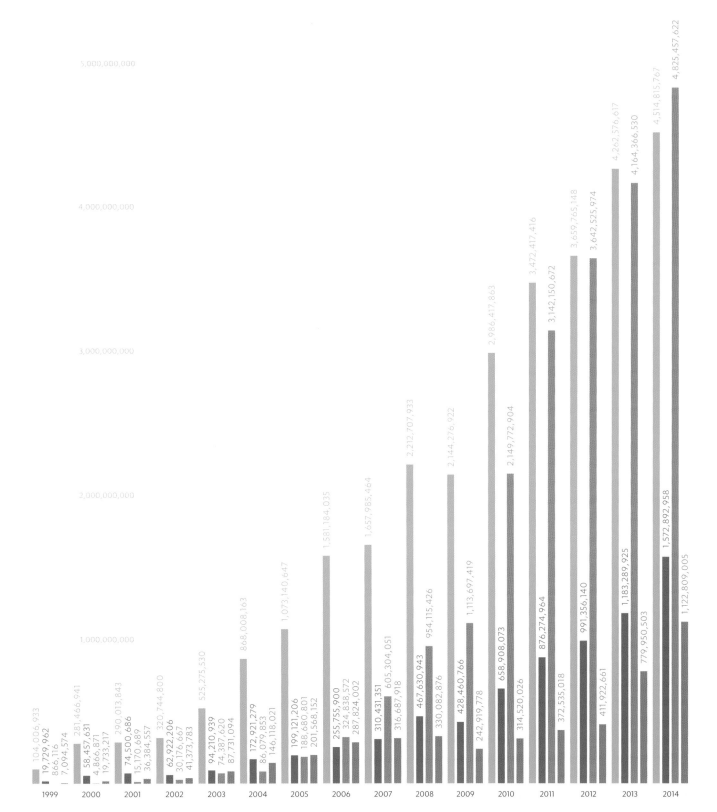

agencies within Defence"; general counsel Phillip Davis joined from Vodafone. In May 2015 finance director Tim Score, who had joined ARM from Rebus Group in 2002, retired; Chris Kennedy, previously CFO at easyJet, joined ARM in the same role and took over over from Tim.

The company expanded physically too, with a new building at its Cambridge headquarters. As always, it followed the distinctive ARM layout, which encourages the casual, informal interactions that have been seen as crucial drivers of innovation since modern capitalism was talked into life in the coffee houses of 18th-century London. Because it's hard enough to get someone to talk to the person at the next desk, and because ARM gets a lot of synergy between the different things ARM people do, this building (construction was planned to begin in late 2015, with the intention that people move in December 2016) will be as open, airy and interconnected as the space allows.

ARM looked to the future in a variety of other ways. One was via the past, when it became the principal sponsor of the Information Age gallery at London's Science Museum. The largest and "most ambitious" of the museum's galleries, the Information Age's permanent exhibit details and explores "innovation in information and communication technologies" over the past two centuries and more. It takes the visitor on a journey from cable to telephone, to radio, to computers, to networks, to the Internet. The gallery was opened on Friday, October 24, 2014 by HM the Queen, who took a small tech-step of her own that day by sending her first tweet. It read: "It is a pleasure to open the Information Age exhibition today at the @ScienceMuseum and I hope people will enjoy visiting. Elizabeth R."

ARM also reached out to young children, a potential next generation of engineers. In early 2013, spurred by a new UK schools curriculum, it became the first major sponsor of a school-based program, Code Club. Introduced from September 2014, it included teaching children the basics of programming. Volunteer programmers run free clubs in primary schools, helping young children learn how to code by showing them how to create their own computer games, animations and websites. ARM provides the course material.

The clubs are small — an average of 14 pupils in each — and free for both the children and the schools. In 2013 ARM employees were running 15 clubs. Across the country there were 1,500 clubs with 22,000 children involved, and 100 new clubs opening each month. In 2014 a further 750 Code Clubs were set up; by the end of 2014, the program was reaching 30,000 children. Over time, Code Club will be rolled out across the UK. "We are confident of reaching half of the UK's primary schools by 2018," said Laura Kirsop, managing director of Code Club UK, in 2014.

ARM is also a major player in a UK primary school program that has links right back to the company's origins. In 2014 it was approached by the BBC to develop technology, as a prime element of its Make it Digital initiative, that would encourage a new generation of coders and engineers. The result was the BBC micro:bit, a collaboration between 29 partners including ARM, Barclays, BBC, element14, Freescale, Lancaster University, Microsoft, Nordic Semiconductor, Samsung, ScienceScope, Technology Will Save Us and the Wellcome Trust.

The micro:bit is a pocket computer, measuring nearly 2 inches square, in a range of colors. It can be used to control other devices; simple coding — getting it to light up its LEDs, for example — can be done in seconds, with no previous experience. "All that's needed is imagination and creativity," as the press release put it. It was created using ARM mbed hardware and software development kits and compiler services. In

BELOW Buddy, the anthropomorphic robot (designed by BlueFrog Robotics), rolls us safely into the future: built to be an affordable home aide to assist with home security, edutainment and caring for the elderly, his inbuilt cameras allow homeowners to check that all is safe while they're away.

The IBM 370/138

The IBM 370/138 had 512K of memory and was announced on the 30th June 1976. It cost $350,000 or was available to lease directly from IBM for $8,730 per month.

It was just one of the models within the System 370 range of computers which evolved over a period of nearly 20 years starting in 1970.

Features:
Standard dual-processor capability. Full support for virtual memory, 128-bit floating point arithmetic.

Operating Systems that would run on the IBM 370 included DOS/VS, OS/VS1, SVS, MVS and VM/370.

the centre for computing history

CHAPTER 7 ... AND BEYOND

its way, it's a 21st-century equivalent of the 1981 BBC Micro computer, which enthused a generation of coders, helping establish the UK's broad base of game designers. That computer, of which 1.5 million were sold, was developed and built by Acorn, of course.

From September 2015 every child in Year 7 (i.e. who is 11 years old) in the UK will get their own micro:bit, for free. Teachers will be coached to work with children, and there will be a feature about it on the BBC's flagship soap opera, EastEnders. At the technical launch on July 7 ARM CEO Simon Segars said: "Technology is now as much a part of childhood as riding a bicycle or kicking a football, but going from user to innovator is something we still need to encourage. The BBC and Acorn Computers, where ARM technology was first created, came together 35 years ago to develop the BBC Micro, and that inspired the engineers now at the forefront of shaping our increasingly connected world. The new BBC micro:bit has even greater potential because it can inspire boys and girls toward a career in technology at a time of unprecedented demand for science and engineering skills across all areas of the global economy."

The micro:bit makes the complex appear simple and straightforward enough for any 11-year-old to use it, while also offering more challenging possibilities to stretch knowledge and skills. Behind its engaging interface, ARM mbed software enables Lancaster University's micro:bit runtime solution. A Microsoft programming interface sits on top of mbed's professional-grade cloud compiler service, which converts the children's programs into micro:bit code. For students who want to develop programming skills, ARM mbed developer tools are available.

ABOVE ARM's work in the 1980s was made possible by pioneering work in computers of the 1950s, '60s and '70s. You can explore the complete story of computing at The Centre for Computing History in Cambridge (above) or at the Computer History Museum in Mountain View, California.

ARM also has a partnership with the Smallpiece Trust, a program working with young teenagers in disadvantaged schools. In collaboration with Smallpiece, Villers Park Educational Trust and Arkwright Scholarships Trust, ARM is one quarter of the "four-way partnership" 2020 Scholars' Program, which is inspiring 300 young people over the age of 14 toward a science, technology, engineering and mathematics (STEM) career, by supporting them through exams and into university.

In late 2014, ARM became one of the three founding partners of the Global Stem Alliance, an initiative set up and steered by the New York Academy of Sciences. GSA's mission is to find the world's best STEM talent and create a global network of promising students and noted scientists to produce a new generation of STEM innovators. It reaches out to 3 million people a year and is committed to increasing that to an alliance of 1 million students in 100 countries by 2020. It runs after-school sessions. Scientist volunteers — 100 to 120 of them a year — go to schools to "spread their love" of biology, physics and technology. "It's a program that lends itself to the fun, sometimes yucky, hands-on stuff of science," said Meghan Groome, executive director of education and public programs at the New York Academy of Sciences. "It's a testament to the character and value of scientists. They really see part of their job as influencing the next generation."

ARM is also involved in SimPrints. Developed out of an ARM-hosted hackathon at The Humanitarian Centre in Cambridge, it offers a solution to the worldwide problem that a third of all children under 5 have no birth certificate or health records. Among ARM's many partners is Zone V, a Cambridge startup founded by Abhi Naha, which develops smartphones for the blind and partially sighted. For each smartphone sold in developed countries, one is made available, free, to a blind woman in India.

In 2013, ARM partnered with Unicef on an 18-month project in Ghana, using Talking Book technology, to educate more than 40,000 people in some of the world's poorest families. Ian Drew: "Unicef has huge reach and we've got a huge ecosystem." Unicef's Literacy Bridge program, developed with the University of Michigan's Department of Electrical Engineering, is based around the Talking Book, which is run by an ARM Cortex-M0. A small and very cheap device, the Talking Book displays simple spoken educational and instructional messages. Hence its capacity to reach the poorest and least educated communities. It helps them learn — and adopt — ways of improving (for example their farming methods and self healthcare) at minimum cost. The aim, says Cliff Schmidt, executive director of Literacy Bridge, is to "dramatically reduce the energy requirements," using ARM technology, and bring the unit cost down to around $10. Already there have been reports of the Talking Book helping African farmers achieve a 48 percent increase in crop yield.

In the short space of 20 years ARM had grown from being a small team, working out of a barn in Cambridgeshire, to become an organization that could share a stage with Unicef. And it had done so by employing the kind of people who, like Ian Drew and Mike Muller, failed O-level English at age 16 but who excelled at other things, such as engineering and marketing. It says as much about ARM as any study of its stats and figures that Ian was offered a job with ARM in 1991, after he'd designed a CPU as an undergraduate at Teesside Polytechnic. After turning Robin Saxby down, he eventually joined Intel as a marketing engineer, working in Singapore, Moscow and Swindon. However, when many years later he decided Intel had become a "utility" that was stagnating and no longer pushing the boundaries of technology, he emailed (the by now) Sir Robin Saxby.

The dream of freedom and mobility

ABOVE The Mercedes-Benz F015 Luxury in Motion autonomous concept car at the 2015 International Consumer Electronics Show.

"You may not remember me," Ian's email began … He took a pay cut to do so, but he joined the company. Such a move was considered a gamble even ten years ago, because while Intel spends an annual $3 billion on promoting itself, ARM, not unintentionally, is well below the radar of nearly everyone. But Ian joined because, he says, he "wanted to change the world." Which is what ARM has done.

Being able to access the Internet on mobiles and tablets has revolutionized so much of people's lives. ARM has played a major role in making email available everywhere, for sub-Saharan farmers being able to check market prices, for the multimillion views of cat videos, and everything else between. "Doing good is good for business" has become a recent motto — long may it continue, because it helps to grow the market.

By 2015, the ARM University Program had more than a thousand universities signed up to access its courses and knowledge. Thousands of students around the world have received the ARM Lab-in-a-Box, a range of six products, each of which contains an ARM University Program Education kit and relevant ARM boards, along with "a full suite" of academic teaching, lab and lecture materials.

As ARM University and ARM chips reach across the world, potential engineers everywhere can gain access to the same level of expertise and rigor needed in-house to help create and further the abilities of people working for ARM. After all, the next generation of entrepreneurs and engineers, who will shape tomorrow's world, have to begin somewhere.

Following the 2014 launch of 64-bit ARM chips, the company continued its drive into the two markets that Intel could claim to "own": desktops and laptops, and

ABOVE Coming full circle from the BBC Micro Model B, in 2015 ARM enables the BBC micro:bit to help a new generation of engineers.

servers. The first is a flat market, but there is a lot of growth and potential in servers. After all, every mobile phone takes up server space. About 12 million servers are being installed each year, on a base of 50 million. ARM is telling investors it will have 20 percent of that market by 2020. As ever, this drive is one of partnership, with ARM looking to its open source architecture to give it the edge over x86 processors. Applied Micro, for example, is leaving its PowerPC past behind and making the HeliX, a 64-bit ARM-compatible embedded processor. At the 2014 ARM TechCon in Santa Clara, California, Applied Micro's CEO, Paramesh Gopi, said, "We're taking our PowerPC heritage and using it as a stepping stone. We're really changing all of our embedded-based business to be an ARM 64-bit-based business."

In 2014 the mobile market was worth $15 billion, the same as for embedded intelligence and enterprise infrastructure. Both markets are predicted to rise to $25 billion by 2020. An industry forecast in 2012 predicted there would be a trillion connected devices worldwide by 2050, when the world's population will be an estimated 9.6 billion. So that's a little over 100 devices for every boy, girl, man and woman on the planet — as many as Lego says of its little plastic bricks.

In the very near future, everything will be connected, not just personal devices but equipment in the home, in schools, in hospitals. The question as far as ARM is concerned, is how to take all of this technology and use it for good? How to use the data correctly? By the end of the decade, there will 50 billion things connected, if not more. If consciousness is what is produced in the relationship between the outside world and the network interactions in the brain, the Internet of Things will have all the ingredients of consciousness, so it is only a matter of time ... Artificial Inteligence with consciousness is perhaps closer to being a reality than at any time. If it does become a reality, there's every chance that it will be powered by an ARM chip. ∎

Mobile phones 1998-2015

ARM CTO Mike Muller's phones from 1998 to 2014 began with a succession of reliable Nokia candybars with a week-plus of battery life. They were followed by a flurry of monochrome Windows mobiles with Outlook integration and a couple of days' use at best. After a brief dalliance with Blackberry he and we have all learned to live and work with the anxiety of the one-day lasting color smartphone.

Nokia 8110
1998

Nokia 6110
1999

Nokia 6110
2000

Nokia 6310
2001

Nokia 6310i
2002

Nokia 6310i
2003

i-mate SP3
2004

i-mate SP5
2006

Blackberry 8110
2008

Apple iPhone 4
2010

Apple iPhone 5
2012

Apple iPhone 6
2014

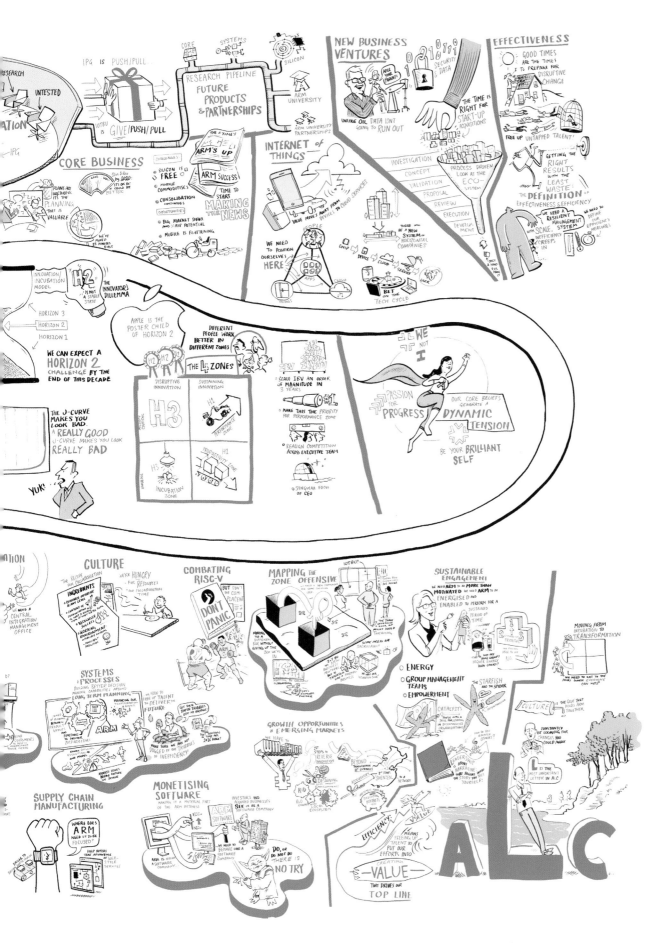

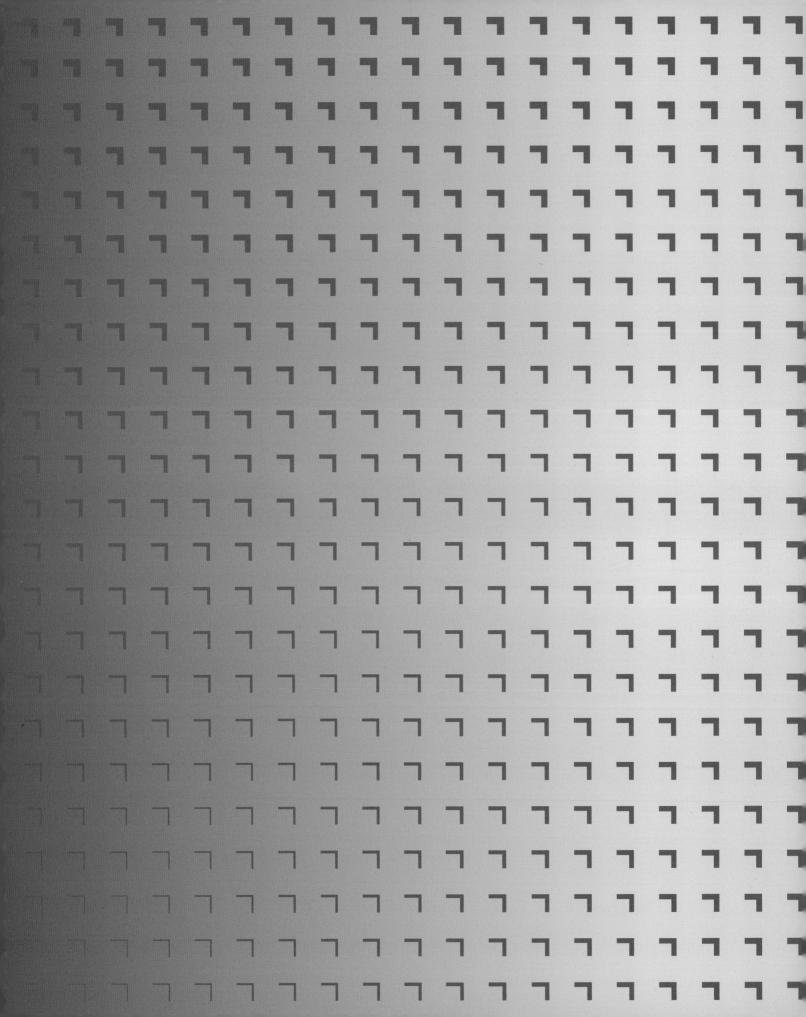

Chapter 8

Close Encounters

Cambridge 1990

In 1983, Acorn occupied the Waterworks and "silver building" (so-named for its metal-clad exterior) on the Fulbourn Road, on the outskirts of Cambridge, which is where Project A began. The "silver building" was intended to be a temporary structure and designed to last for only 10 years, during which time it was hoped that a new science park would be built up the hill behind it.

After three years at the Barn in Swaffham, in 1994 ARM moved into to the old Acorn site. In 1999, we built ARM1, renamed the "silver building" as ARM2, and returned the Waterworks to Cambridge Water. We have slowly expanded the campus since then, and took over what became ARM3 and then the next building on the site which, in honor of Larry Tesler, we named ARM6. We've now come nearly full circle, and are overseeing the construction of two new offices (with planning permission for a third) on the hill behind the old "silver building," which will be demolished and the site turned into a car park. It lasted for more than three times the lifetime it was intended to have, though — kind of like the ARM7TDMI. ▮

LEFT (far) The facade of the ARM1 building and (near) the main entrance to ARM1.

San Jose, CA 1991

The history of ARM's presence in Silicon Valley spans several offices across three cities and began in early 1990, in Los Gatos, south of San Jose, near the foothills of the Santa Cruz Mountains. The second office opened when we had grown to about six people, primarily in sales, in a building famous for its massive wooden doors and directly adjacent to where Netflix was founded. In true ARM fashion, the Los Gatos office was within stumbling distance of a sports bar where many a "meeting" was held.

With the acquisition of Artisan Components in December 2004, ARM relocated to Artisan's headquarters in Sunnyvale, very near the former Moffett Field Air Force base. When staff levels grew to the point that a second office was needed, unfortunately the only site available was about a half mile away, and entailed splitting off many functions to a second location. In January 2009, though, ARM moved to the present site on Rose Orchard Way, at the very top of San Jose, situated near the adjacent cities of Santa Clara, Sunnyvale, Milpitas and Alviso. Originally a Lockheed Martin warehouse, the building was gutted and transformed into an open, airy working environment specifically designed to promote collaboration. This larger office consolidated all Bay Area staff in one building and is now home to approximately 300 employees. ▪

BELOW The ARM San Jose office — it has the world's largest ARM logo on its roof. You can see it as you take off from San Jose Airport, apparently.

Maidenhead 1992

It's true, the ARM Maidenhead office has great links to Heathrow airport (30 minutes away), an enviable town center location and beautiful scenery along the River Thames within just a 2-minute walk, but this isn't the reason why we have a presence here.

Actually, the fact that Sir Robin Saxby has a house just a 10-minute drive away and wanted an office close by was the main factor behind our M4 corridor existence. But we're still here, not least because dear Sir Robin signed a 25-year lease without a break clause. Do come and visit if you ever need office time, we'll always find you a desk. ▮

ABOVE The Maidenhead office — still here after almost 25 years. Thanks, Sir Robin!

Shin-Yokohama
1994

ARM K.K. was originally established on September 1, 1994 at KSP in Musashi Mizonokuchi, where we worked until 1998. Then we relocated to the Zuken Building in Shin-Yokohama for three years. In 2001, the company moved to the Daini Ueno Building in Shin-Yokohama, and thrived there until 2012, enjoying annual mbed festivals in the office. In 2012 we moved into the Shin-Yokohama Squire Building where, since 2013, more than 100 people have attended our now twice-yearly mbed festivals. The ARM K.K. office has been properly recognized as a sacred place. ■

TOP   ARM K.K. believe that if there is no music, then there is no life!
ABOVE   ARM K.K. discuss developing the ECO train to save the Earth.

Austin, TX 1997

The Austin Design Center is British born, but has been Texas bred — it was initially formed in 1997 when Dave Jaggar, one of the top inventors at ARM, came to Austin as the first of many invaders to land in Austin with microprocessor talent. By 2008, the Austin office had grown to about 120 people, and moved into 42,000 sq ft at The Park, which sits on the edge of a large greenbelt with running and bike trails just a short walk from its front door. In 2015 the Austin Design Center has about 400 people working in many different teams. In July we moved to a brand new facility called Encino Trace, with its own on-site café and outdoor amenities that offer something for everyone. The Austin Design Center has its roots in microprocessors, and in 2005 became a multi-design site when we formed a team to work on memories and standard cell design as part of the Artisan acquisition. Today, ARM Austin is a microcosm of ARM, with teams and representatives from many of its businesses and functional groups.

ABOVE   The home of ARM Austin since 2015, the brand new Encino Trace.

Seoul 1997

ARM Korea's founding ceremony was held at the Ramada Renaissance hotel on June 5, 1997, with Sam Kim (who joined in April) and Jay Leem (joined May) meeting with Andy Lee and Susan Kim. The fifth ARM Korea employee was hired in 2001. Because the word "arm" is a homonym to the Korean word for "cancer," there was much debate on how ARM Korea's name should be submitted to the Korean Government registry. After much internal debate, it was decided that the official Korean name would be a spelled-out version of the original: "Ay-Ar-Em Korea."

After a difficult beginning, ARM Korea's fortunes turned in the middle of 1998 when Sam Kim, while driving over a bridge across the North-Han River, received a call from a Samsung executive who asked if the proposal of ARM9TDMI/ARM920T provided to them a while ago was still valid. Subsequently, the ARM9TDMI/ARM920T license with Samsung SLSI was signed on December 24, 1998. That was the start of the strategic relationship with Samsung SLSI. Originally begun as a sales office, ARM Korea now also covers segment marketing and application engineering. We have four times the number of employees we began with (that's 16). ▮

ABOVE ARM Korea's HQ in Seoul.
BELOW ARM Korea's staff on an outing, Seoul, 2015.

Paris 1998

In 1998, when ARM decided to invest in France, Eric Lalardie, the first employee, worked from home until we took a small office for two people in an incubator building called Promopôle. IKEA cabinets on wheels were bought to allow us to move the office within the same building several times, and they've served us well. The moves were achieved in less than a day. Eventually — with funds from the city to assist us — the office will be renovated and modernized.

We here at ARM Paris service customers across Europe, from Portugal to Russia, and places as far apart as Africa, India and the Arctic Circle. Which means that, although there are nine of us in the office, often Karin our assistant is left alone, because everyone else is away on sales business. She says it's much quieter then. ▌

RIGHT   The entry hall for ARM Paris offices in the Promopôle building — perfect for wheeling office furniture around.

ABOVE ARM Seattle's entry, conveniently located, although the building isn't actually in Seattle.

Seattle, WA 1999

Opened in 1999, the Seattle office (which has never actually been in Seattle itself) was originally founded to develop a relationship with Microsoft, and specifically focused on Windows CE and Windows Mobile. At one point our address was on Microsoft Way, on the Microsoft campus. However, technically it was the smallest and most uncomfortable office (triangular in shape, with a pole in one corner) in the ARM family. Back then, people visited and took photographs out of a sense of awe (we think). We had to share a small work table, since nothing else would fit — but we were lucky; Intel's Windows CE representative worked in a remodeled broom cardboard. Thankfully we've expanded, and now we have colleagues who work in strategic alliances, segment marketing, new business ventures and sales. Most of them even have their own desks.

Today, ARM's engineering, marketing and senior executive teams regularly visit the Seattle area, and it has become a desirable destination on the West Coast. ▮

San Diego, CA 1999

ARM San Diego was opened in 1999, by Andy Murphy (who left ARM in 2005). He'd arrived in the area initially to call on Qualcomm, and decided a local presence was needed. Shortly after it opened, Andy was joined by Antonio Viana, who relocated from Los Gatos in 2000, and Richard Meacham, who came to ARM from the UK in 2002. By 2015, the ARM San Diego office had grown to 14 people, covering a range of roles: executive management, sales, FAE, marketing, admin, the Wireless Connectivity BU and the IoTBU. ARM San Diego epitomizes the San Diego culture of being a "laid back" environment, while always getting the job done. We are definitely a "work hard, play hard" office. When you come to San Diego, please be advised that a "ball fight" can break out at any moment. ▮

LEFT   ARM San Diego offices are a health and safety officer's nightmare.

Kfar Netter 2000

ARM Israel started out with a single-person sales office in November 2000, based in Kfar Saba. In July 2015, ARM acquired Sansa Security, with whom it had worked for over 10 years. The Sansa Security team are — of course — proud to now be a part of ARM (as they told everyone on the day that the photo below was taken). The acquisition represented a significant milestone in ARM's evolution, providing Silicon to Application security expertise, and establishing an engineering presence in Israel.

ARM Israel is now a full engineering design center based north of Tel Aviv in Kfar Netter, contributing to the road maps of both the Systems and Software group and the IoT Business Unit. We look forward to contributing to the next 25 years of success at ARM. ▮

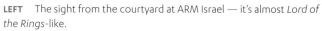

LEFT The sight from the courtyard at ARM Israel — it's almost *Lord of the Rings*-like.
BELOW The whole office gathered to celebrate the announcement of the acquisition of Sansa Security by ARM, July 2015.

Sophia Antipolis 2000

ABOVE Our current building — just 300 meters from where we used to be.

In 1995, a startup called EuroMIPS Systems was developing IPs, SoCs and standard-cell libraries for TI, and had acquired a serious expertise in smartcards and security in general. In 1997, EuroMIPs was working for Texas Instruments on a European project to create the first smartcard based on a 32-bit RISC processor (guess which one!) in partnership with Gemplus, now known as Gemalto. Slightly less than three years later, two Englishmen, Warren East and Bill Parsons (who was trying to hide the blue, three-lettered logo he had on his T-shirt), came to visit and announced that we had become ARM employees. They also told us that our office had officially become the "ARM e-commerce design center". ▮

Rockingham Court

Sheffield 2000

Infinite Designs was an eight-person consultancy startup, spun-out from Sheffield University in 1998. Working on anything and everything, from training services to a solid-state video camera for motorbike racing, Infinite Designs was acquired by ARM on April 1, 2000.

ARM Sheffield has occupied three different buildings, having grown from eight employees to over 100 in 15 years. So far we have taped out: 31 chips, 7 technology nodes 0.18 um to 16 nm, 6 foundries, 34 different CPU cores: ARM7TDMI up to A57. We also hold an annual bowling trip, annual TeamARM bike ride, various annual charity events such as Red Nose Day, Sports Relief and Movember. But we really enjoy paper plane flying competitions and visiting the pub on a Friday.

TOP   ARM Sheffield in-house entertainments tend toward the loud. Here Chris Heald, Samuel Clare, the significantly named Andy Tune and Damian Richardson try out their best impersonation of Pulp for their workmates.
ABOVE   ARM Sheffield has more than 100 people spread over the first, second and fourth floors of this building.

Taipei, Hsinchu 2000

The ARM Hsinchu design center (colloquially known as HDC) is located in Taiwan. It was established in September 2011 when it was decided that we needed an engineering presence close to our ever-expanding customer base in Asia. ARM has had a presence in Taipei, Taiwan, since 2000; it is now primarily focused on sales and marketing activities, not engineering. The Hsinchu design center was sponsored by Simon Segars, then GM of ARM Physical IP Division, and reported directly to Dipesh Patel, then VP of Engineering for PIPD. The office is located in the Hsinchu Science Park, an area set up by the Taiwanese government in 1980. It was deliberately chosen to be across the road from the headquarters of TSMC; no way we would be out of sight and out of mind. Frequent visitors often remarked on the strange smell emanating from somewhere in the basement. We never did find out what it was, but we assumed it wasn't deadly gasses leaking from the silicon fab across the road. The other often-remarked-on feature was the piped music that first sounded to remind you that it was lunchtime, and again to get you back to work. Given that the Taiwanese will never miss a meal, I have no idea why music was required to remind everybody to eat. Happily, in May 2015 we finally got to leave the foul smells and even fouler lunch music behind, and moved to modern premises more in keeping with ARM's global office standards. We are still within spitting distance of TSMC HQ, but the music has stopped.

TOP An ARM Taiwan office outing to TSMC, whose office is just across the road from the new Hsinchu HQ.

ABOVE ARM Taiwan announces the launch of their fourth CPU design center in Hsinchu by giving it the thumbs up, June 2014.

Blackburn 2001

In February 2001, ARM acquired the seven-person engineering team of Noral Micrologics Ltd and moved us into a newly built office located in Blackburn with easy access to the M65 motorway. Since then the site has expanded, and by 2015 hosted 24 staff developing debug and trace hardware units (e.g. DSTREAM). We're a major contributor to the DS-5 Debugger and often help IP teams with support of IP at early stages in the development cycle.

One of the office highlights is making use of our open plan outdoor canteen (bottom left), which allows lunch to be purchased and brought back to the office, enabling us to enjoy the fine Lancashire weather all year round. It has become common to engage in playing chess and other such stimulating mental challenges during lunch breaks. Note the northern tradition of polishing the road surfaces to make it appear as if it may be wet outside.

TOP   ARM Blackburn's TeamARM charity bowling squad, raising money for Derian House Children's Hospice, l-r: Stuart Hirons, Sean Wood, Kamil Pawlowski, Tania Brankov, Richard Yearsley, Andy Lee-Smith, Alan Parker.
ABOVE   ARM Blackburn's outdoor canteen, in typical shining weather.

Beijing, Shanghai, Shenzhen
2002

ARM China's first office was established in 2002, with two employees. After much expansion the current Shanghai office was opened 10 years later, hosting 157 colleagues spread over two floors. The Beijing office was opened on September 7, 2004, and faces Peking University, one of the best universities in China. When not working, we all enjoy playing football, basketball, badminton, billiards, and we organize an annual charity marathon. The Shenzhen office started with one person on June 11, 2008, but has grown to 14; we moved into a new building in 2014.

ARM China support a number of charities, including tree planting, Angel Mom, wheelchair donation and support for the disadvantaged children of western China. ▮

TOP   The ARM China Shenzhen office.
CENTER   The Vice Minister of the Ministry of Industry and Information Technology of the People's Republic of China, Mr. Huai Jinpeng, participates in a contract-signing ceremony between ARM CEO Simon Segars and Spreadtrum CEO Li Liyou in Beijing, March 24, 2015.
LEFT   The ARM China Beijing office on a day out.

ABOVE ARM Irvine, possibly the smallest in
the company, l-r: Mel Butler, Paul Manfrini,
Rob Telson, Dawn Hill.

Irvine, CA 2004

ARM's Irvine Office came via the Axys Design Automation acquisition in July 2004;
Dawn Hill was the first employee. Axys was a modeling company with products that
eventually led to the SOC designer. There are five of us at Irvine, and we've laughed at
the 5,000+ earthquakes we've had in the last decade. We had fewer laughs about the
major flood and three major wildfires, but we experience a drought every other year
and our average temperature in the Irvine area is 26 C during the day and 11 C at night.
So we're hardy. The office is 9 km due east of the Pacific Ocean and a short drive to
the world's most beautiful coastal region, Laguna Beach, CA. The Happiest Place on
Earth, also known as Disneyland, is a short 13 km drive north of our office. We feel very
strongly that if we had to choose between the Happiest Place on Earth or the Most
Beautiful Beaches in the World, we would spend our free time at the latter. But that's
just us.

Bangalore, Noida
2004

ARM India began its journey as part of Artisan Components in 2002; we recruited 45 employees primarily for Physical IP Design. Most of them were fresh grads so we trained all of them in Sunnyvale, CA, for six to nine months. With ARM's acquisition of Artisan in 2004, what started as a team of 40 is now a 500-strong organization. The very first batch that we recruited as ARM India in 2005 for the processor design division, also spent about 6 months in Cambridge for technical training and cross-cultural learning. As we increased in number, we were forced to move to our fourth location in Bangalore, which also happens to be ARM's first LEED Gold-certified green office.

ARM India opened its second office at Noida in 2013, to augment our Memory Design team. Noida, an integrated residential, industrial and institutional township, is located on the outskirts of New Delhi, India's capital city, on the banks of River Yamuna in the National Capital Region. ARM Noida began as an exclusive center for PDG group, with a primary mission of development and support of Memory Compiler IPs. The center, which started with 12 people, now boasts more than 60, among them established employees, consultants and interns. The ARM Noida center has ramped up quickly and garnered management trust and support with several important product deliveries to key customers like Samsung, UMC, SMIC and AMD. We sometimes have to work in difficult conditions — for instance, in May 2015 everyone was working as usual when suddenly we felt the earth shaking. We rushed to the safest place and all eventually became still; the earthquake passed without damage. ▍

TOP AND CENTER   ARM Noida bond over celebrations and meals.
BOTTOM LEFT   The offices of ARM India in Bangalore.
BOTTOM RIGHT   The Noida building opened in 2013.

TOP ARM Munich supports the Oktoberfest — and also has several sports teams who climb mountains, ski and run together.
ABOVE The current office, across the road from the original Keil Software office, in TechnoPark1, Grasbrunn.

Munich 2004

ARM Germany is located in the TechnoPark1 Grasbrunn, a business area that was built between 1987 and 1990. Grasbrunn is a village on the boarder of Munich with good infrastructure — the office is close to public transport, the autobahn, airport and the Munich Exhibition Centre. The office is a result of mergers: two acquisitions (AXYS, Keil) and the original ARM Munich office. AXYS was acquired in 2004; the technology is today a part of the ARM FastModels. AXYS was originally located in Aachen, but the office was closed in 2009. Some key engineers moved to Munich and are now part of the DSG engineering team. Keil Software was founded in 1985 with a focus on developing microcontroller tools; it was acquired in 2005. The Keil technology is the foundation for the Microcontroller Development Kit (MDK). Keil Software moved in 1988 to TechnoPark, where we only needed to occupy the first and second floors of the building. Today, the ARM Office is just across the street and occupies about twice the space — now including basement and ground floor. We are surrounded by trees. ▌

Plano, TX 2005

The ARM Plano office was opened in 1985 as the initial US base for Keil Tools, an industry leader in C compilers, debuggers, simulators and real-time operating systems. The office maintained exceptional sales and support teams and a warehouse that serviced all of the Americas. In 2005 the Plano Keil office became part of ARM with the Keil Tools acquisition. Today it is a hub for ARM's support and inside sales teams. It also functions as a regional hub for those working in and around the Dallas Texas area.

The Plano team is an energetic group of people, many of whom have worked together for a long time, but we still have a great time hanging out. Back in the early days we used to hand write serial numbers on cards, and track them in a notebook.

ABOVE The HQ of ARM Plano, Texas — they have the highest level of phone traffic per capita than any other ARM office, apparently.

Grenoble 2006

The Grenoble site was built in 2004 and hosted SOISIC, a 2001 startup spin-off from the LETI research laboratory based in the city, founded by Eric Dupont-Nivet and Jean-Luc Pelloie. SOISIC was initially created to become a fabless company targeting RF applications such as Bluetooth, Wi-Fi, Zigbee, etc. using SOI processes. The company originally had two sites: one in Paris with an RF design team, another in Grenoble with a digital design team. Several testchips were designed and manufactured by different partners: OKI, IBM. The lack of SOI Physical IP availability led the founders to focus and re-orient the company purely on SOI Physical IP development. The RF design activity was dropped. SOISIC then became the only company offering SOI standard cell libraries, memory compilers and I/O. When the SOI volume market never showed up, limiting the company's development and growth, it led ultimately to the 2006 sale to ARM. Since then, SOI physical IP has been developed on several process generations (45, 32, 22, 14 nm), mainly for IBM. ▌

ABOVE   Having fun at ARM Grenoble usually means having a nice luncheon with champagne — as our future CEO discovered, when he celebrated the Grenoble office extension opening in 2010.

BELOW   ARM Grenoble's office was extended in 2010; in 2015 it was home to 42 people, mostly in the physical design group. It's at the foot of the Alps, which is why it's snowing.

Šentjernej 2006

ABOVE   The tiny HQ of ARM Slovenia in Šentjernej.

The ARM Slovenia office is situated in Šentjernej, a small town in the southeastern part of Slovenia. The office is inside a 2002 building (owned by the town's current mayor), located in the industrial zone. It has a meeting room and two work rooms, and is one of the smallest ARM offices, with only five engineers working on development tools for microcontrollers (MDK-ARM product).

ARM opened the office in 2006 after it acquired Keil in October 2005; the Keil engineers working in Slovenia joined ARM. The team has a daily routine of going out for a half-hour coffee break in the nearby bar where it socializes and discusses various topics. ▐▌

TOP   ARM Norway's home in Trondheim since 2012 used to be a bank. Their previous office used to be a slaughterhouse.

ABOVE   After ARM Norway moved into their renovated premises, a caretaker found 1 million kroner left in one of the bank's old safe-deposit boxes.

Trondheim 2006

The ARM Norway office in Trondheim was officially opened when ARM acquired Falanx Microsystems AS in 2006. Falanx had been founded by five students out of the Norwegian University of Science and Technology in 2001, with a plan to develop and sell graphics processors. After first targeting PCs they soon refocused toward mobile phones and other highly integrated systems, under the Mali brand. When ARM acquired Falanx it employed about 20 people and had already had success with its first commercial graphics processor, Mali-55. After the acquisition the office in Trondheim grew rapidly, and the old Falanx facilities at Bakke Bridge quickly became cramped. In 2008 we moved into newly refurbished facilities in Gryta 2B. The building went by the name "The Slaughter House" because it was actually the listed building of the Trondheim slaughterhouse (from 1919 to 1980). One meat hook hanging from the ceiling is still preserved and visible. The Graphics division of ARM grew rapidly between 2008 and 2011, leading to major investment in Trondheim to expand both the hardware and software engineering teams. More engineers meant a need for more space, and in the spring of 2012 ARM signed a lease for a new building that previously had hosted a bank. Extensive renovations were made and most of the building was completely refurbished. In the process, a caretaker found about a million Norwegian kroner in the vault. ▮

Lund 2009

The ARM Lund office was founded in late 2009, when ARM acquired the Lund-based video IP company Logipard. At the time of acquisition Logipard had a 15-person team mostly consisting of local engineering talent. Six years later, the responsibilities of the Lund site have grown significantly and the site is now an important part of both the video and GPU development in MPG. We now have almost 90 employees in the office, originating from more than 14 different countries. In the spring of 2014 we moved into our current offices located in the Ideon Research Park in the northern part of Lund.

TOP ARM Sweden HQ since 2014, at the Ideon Research Park, Lund.
CENTER ARM Sweden powering their Dragonboat in a race, l-r: drummer unknown, Richard Bramley, Anders Fyhn, Reimar Doffinger, Staffan Gadd, Henrik Ohlsson, Charles Xu, Anders Karlsson, Jonas Henriksson, Yunus Okmen, Abeesh Mahaveer, Mathias Palmqvist.
RIGHT ARM Sweden's serious foosball players, Erik Eksborg and Henrik Hoglind battle it out.

Oulu 2013

Despite the long history between ARM and Nokia — once one of the largest handset manufacturers in the world — the only ARM office in Finland was opened in 2013 when ARM acquired the small Finnish mesh networking and web technology software startup Sensinode to boost its IoT offering. The current office was purpose-built back in the 1990s for a local technology company, and Sensinode moved in during May 2012. The location — in the industrial suburbs of Oulu — might not be the most exotic but the office does make up for it with other amenities. Due to the rapid increase in personnel since opening, the current plan is to move into new premises some time in 2016. Although Oulu has only approximately 190,000 inhabitants it has become one of the hubs for wireless communications research in Europe and has a booming startup scene. The office staff consists almost exclusively of IoTBU software engineers.

We are the northernmost ARM office in the world, but we're very friendly and welcome all visitors with open arms. The office has a unique feature that is considered to be an essential part of a Finnish culture: a sauna. It's in regular use for office sauna evenings that usually see people playing table tennis, Rock Band (the console game) and singing karaoke. ▮

TOP   Part of the Oulu office (with the frequent travelers missing).
ABOVE   The very discreet entrance to the Oulu office.

Manchester 2014

This design center was founded on July 21, 2014, and is an APD compiler team within DSG. The founding team of nine have worked together for almost 15 years, initially as part of a dynamic binary translation startup spun out of Manchester University called Transitive — it most famously delivered Rosetta to Apple, ushering in the new era of Intel Macs. The team of 14 in 2015 is set to rise to over 20 by the end of 2016. We are on the fourth floor of a 10-story block built in the 1950s, recently renovated and located in the very heart of the city. On the ground floor is a Canadian diner that serves Oreo milkshakes and a sweet doughnut steak burger Scooby-snack. Every meal comes with a free trip to the hospital. The office space is 3,000 sq ft with a current capacity for 26, and was designed from scratch according to our specific requirements. We moved into the renovated office space on January 19, 2014. We have meeting rooms named after locations from sci-fi, and each one has a model representing its name: for example Gallifrey has a Tardis containing intergalactic sweets, and Dagobah is home to Master Yoda, who is available for Jedi training every Tuesday and Thursday at 7:00 p.m. Many of us have completed our training but some still need to return ...

We are a young tight-knit family with an informal startup culture (but without the Nerf guns). We try to be open and sociable and interact with the rest of ARM, whenever possible, to stay connected to the Mothership. We also believe in equal rights for extraterrestrials.

LEFT ARM Manchester HQ. In 1996 a terrorist bomb exploded in Manchester city center. Thankfully nobody was hurt, but much was destroyed and had to be rebuilt. It's now new and shiny, and full of beautiful people.

Galway 2014

In 2001, Duolog (founded in 1999) set up its "West Coast" office in the beautiful city of Galway — a vibrant and fun city on the Atlantic coast of Ireland. The main focus of the Galway office was the development of Duolog's tooling — the Socrates platform designed to solve the SoC/IP integration problem. In August 2014, ARM acquired Duolog. The teams from the Galway office are currently involved with producing innovative ARM IP tooling solutions to be used for our next-generation IP, including producing a new ARM IP Catalog within Socrates. Just so everybody knows, one of the rules of the Galway office is that if you are returning from a trip, you must bring back some local delicacies: biscuits, sweets, etc. In between visits, Brian and Stephen partake in their masterchef war and keep us well-fed on flapjacks and cake. To relax, we go kart racing, boating and greyhound racing, before eventually winding down in one or many of the great pubs in the city. Not every day, of course.

ABOVE ARM Ireland's splendid West Coast HQ in beautiful, sunny Galway.

BELOW ARM Ireland staff tuck into plates of delicacies from abroad.

ABOVE The Budapest team, l-r: Gabor Molnar, Tibor Marton, Attila Hudak, Attila Vida, Viktor Szentgyorgyi, Norbert Santa, Balazs Bodis, Imre-Attila Mados, Endre Papp, Cesar Matias, Gabor Moricz, Jozsef Andras Ferencz, Tamas Olaszi, Daniel Misak, Tamas Gyimesi, Csaba Kiss, Tamas Fulop, Zoltan Parragh, Peter Falucskai, Laszlo Vagasi, Maria Dalnoki, Peter Vari, Gergely Kiss.

Budapest 2014

Duolog Technologies Ltd. was founded in 1999 and is based in Dublin, Ireland. Its Budapest office was opened in 2003, with about 10 engineers. This site mainly focused on design and verification services (on IP, sub-chip or SoC level) for various customers, including Texas Instruments and Cadence. In 2015 the Budapest office has 38 colleagues, most of them engineers working for SSG and PEG. The Budapest office was visited by a delegation of the Irish parliament and the Irish ambassador in 2013, and to honor Irish tradition we are organizing a 12-pub tour at the end of 2015. We train by consuming an average of 150 liters of drinking water every week. There are two colleagues at ARM Budapest with the same name: Gergely Kiss.

ABOVE The Budapest office, where 38 people work, play csosco at lunchtime, and drink lots of water.

TOP   Members of the ARM Deerfield Beach team on Day 1.
ABOVE   The current ARM Deerfield office on 350 Fairway Drive in Deerfield Beach, Florida.

Deerfield, FL 2015

The team in Deerfield Beach, Florida, is happy and proud to be a part of ARM. We started in June 2009 as Sunrise Micro Devices working from offices at the back of a small strip shopping center, right next to the dumpster. We fondly referred to this as our "World-Wide Headquarters." At the time, there were only seven of us, and we paid the bills by providing design services to government and commercial entities. With ARM investment in March 2013 came growth and a move to our current office in Deerfield Beach. With a team of about 25 engineers, we are able to produce complete integrated radio IP solutions for the wireless marketplace. Our office is located in the coastal community of Deerfield Beach on the southeast coast of Florida. It is part of the metropolitan area that includes Miami, Fort Lauderdale and Palm Beach. The main draw to the area is the warm weather and the beautiful beaches, which are about five minutes from our office. The culture of the office is decidedly startup. We worked a lot of long hours to bring our first product to market. Late nights and pizza dinners in the lab are common. High trust and low ego are how we try to operate. That said, there is always time for play.

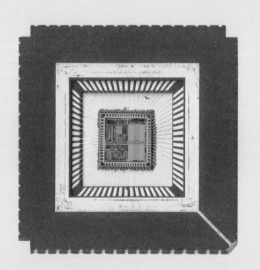